The
Marketing Planning
Workbook

Also Available for Readers

Exclusive Disk Offer

The charts in this workbook are intended for readers to fill in as they develop their own marketing plans. For those who would like to use the charts in a team situation, there is a simple disk available that allows readers to print exactly the same forms in A4 size. Ideal for team working, overhead projection, in-house training or for lectures, this gives the reader the opportunity to use the forms again and again.

The disk contains the following:

- the forms filled in as examples
- the forms blank and protected for printing
- simple instructions for printing these forms
- cross references to the book

The disk is available in $3\frac{1}{2}$ inch size. Price, including postage, packing and VAT, on application.

To order a copy please contact Customer Services, ITBP, Andover, Hants, SP10 5BE. Order telephone hotline: 01264 342923 quoting ref. no. 1861520123

Or for further information contact: Francesca Weaver on 0171 497 1422.

By the same authors,
Sally Dibb and Lyndon Simkin,
available from Routledge:

The Market Segmentation Workbook: Target Marketing for Marketing Managers

The Marketing Casebook: Cases and Concepts

The
Marketing Planning
Workbook

Effective Marketing for Marketing Managers

Sally Dibb, Lyndon Simkin and John Bradley

London and New York

First published 1996
by Routledge
11 New Fetter Lane, London EC4P 4EE

Simultaneously published in the USA and Canada
by Routledge
29 West 35th Street, New York, NY 10001

Typeset in Plantin Light by Solidus (Bristol) Limited
Printed and bound in Great Britain by
Biddles Ltd, Guildford and King's Lynn

British Library Cataloguing in Publication Data
A catalogue record for this book is available from the British Library

Library of Congress Cataloging in Publication Data
Dibb, Sally, 1963
    The marketing planning workbook : effective marketing for
marketing managers / Sally Dibb, Lyndon Simkin, and John Bradley.
Simultaneously published in the United States and Canada.
Includes bibliographical references (p.).
ISBN 0–415–11891–3
1. Marketing–Planning.   I. Simkin, Lyndon, 1961–
II. Bradley, John, 1952–   III. Title.   IV. Series.
HF5415. 13.D477   1996   95–30550
658.8'02–dc20   CIP

ISBN 0–415–11891–3

For Becky, Jamie and Abby

'Without marketing planning no company truly succeeds: many companies fail to survive'

Marketing planning creates a focus on the customer, an awareness of competitors' strategies, and an understanding of market trends.

Strategies maximise opportunities and sidestep principal threats. Marketing and sales programmes stress the company's advantages and convey a coherent message to customers, distributors and the marketplace.

Marketing planning as a process of analysis, thought and action is essential for business survival and long-term success. Marketing planning is no academic exercise; it has to become integral to the company's management style and ethos.

Contents

Figures

porate Marketing Director, JCB Sales

Marketing and Marketing

ential and often quoted papers ever written
ents on the great pressure to 'move the
on'. Marketing he comments, 'being a more
x process, gets ignored'. Can this be one of
rent decline of British manufacturing? Are
ompanies more sophisticated in their use of
d process? This topic could generate great
ademic circles without coming to a concrete

been relatively little research into this subject,
tive of the problem. Research undertaken
that the British are less sophisticated in their
trategic and marketing planning than the
e investigation of Japanese Marketing strat-
ket' by Doyle *et al.* (1986)[1] showed that
ating in Britain had a much better grasp of
strategies than their British competitors.
e companies implemented strategies based
g and positioning their products in their
ish, on the other hand, took a homogenous
y ignored their competitors and focused on
ved productivity as a source of competitive

stomer or market orientation is spreading
under the guise of Total Quality Manage-
roduction line concept of a chain of internal
ltimately leads through the factory gate and
ributors, consumers and competitors. Total
rinciples and other production-orientated
Functional Deployment (QFD) mirror the
marketing concept but do not present a framework for sorting the
wood from the trees in increasingly complex and volatile market
situations. A well-structured, objective and comprehensive marketing

planning programme does bring order to the chaos of markets and provides a clear sense of purpose for a business.

This workbook explains the marketing planning process and activities, first explaining the concepts behind marketing planning, then working through the various analysis and planning steps in a logical sequence. The proformas have been developed in conjunction with some of the leading brands in Europe and have proved to be practical and effective.

In JCB, marketing planning and the process at the heart of this workbook have been used to good effect over a number of years. It is important to note here that marketing planning *per se* (or indeed the marketing plan) is not an end in itself. Rather the adoption of a formal process should be seen as the means of providing a clear structure to existing efforts. A marketing plan is the framework within which the needs of the organisation and the needs of the target markets are defined and the necessary actions prescribed to meet those needs.

Marketing planning as a process helps individuals and organisations to:

- understand markets and anticipate market trends
- understand the needs and wants of a range of customers and potential customers
- combat and beat competitors
- understand the organisation's strengths and weaknesses relative to competitors
- develop competitive products/services
- test planning assumptions
- set marketing objectives and strategies
- structure and balance the marketing mix
- create maximum personnel motivation
- optimise the use of scarce resources – both financial and people
- position the company and product range so that stability and growth can be maintained in volatile markets.

All too frequently the term 'marketing' is used as a substitute for advertising or sales promotion. Companies or even political parties are described as being successful because they have discovered 'marketing', when in effect they have been self-promoters.

Marketing is too big a subject to be defined in a single way. This is partly because the marketing concept or philosophy positively encourages us to take a very broad view of our situation and the external influences that can impact on our plans and action.

The marketing concept or philosophy is defined by Philip Kotler of The Kellogg Business School thus:

> The marketing concept holds that the key to achieving organisational goals lies in determining the needs and wants of target markets and delivering the desired satisfaction more efficiently and effectively than the competition.

This statement introduces the key actors in the marketing planning process:

- the organisation or company;
- goals or objectives;
- consumers (markets are people not products); and
- competitors.

Plus, it highlights the key elements of marketing planning:

- targeting;
- establishing customers' needs;
- strategy;
- implementation; and
- control.

This book develops these concepts and explains a proven process for analysing and planning in complex circumstances: analyses are explained and guidance given for their understanding; strategy components are discussed and instruction provided; the required programmes for successful implementation are illustrated and direction offered for their construction.

It is unusual in textbooks to draw a distinction between the marketing concept or philosophy and the process of marketing planning. Indeed most texts assume these are the province of a central marketing function. A better way of considering and explaining 'marketing' in a modern context is to relate the marketing concept, process and function to the organisation as a whole, be it large or small. However, the most benefit from marketing planning can be gained when the whole 'team' contributes to the plan and its implementation. This is equally true in a manufacturing or service environment.

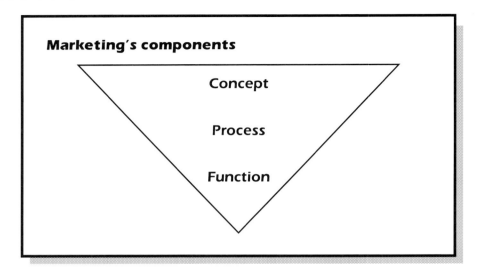

In the schematic representation the breadth of the triangle represents the number of team members involved.

As with TQM, the whole team has to understand and 'buy into' the marketing *concept* for planning, and indeed marketing, to be effective. There is a senior management responsibility to provide training and motivation. Not all the team, however, will be involved in the planning *process*, although a broad range of people will be. People from purchasing through to sales should work together to produce and implement the marketing plan.

Finally a relatively small group of people will make up the marketing *function*. Their role is typically to facilitate the planning process and to implement elements of the plan – marketing research, new product development, pack design and advertising for example. In very small teams or businesses, there may not even be a formal marketing function. In these circumstances the role may be filled by the general manager.

Having drawn a distinction between the marketing concept, process and function we can develop a model of market structure and expand the list of actors and planning elements.

Michael Porter of Harvard Business School developed a model of 'forces driving industry competition':

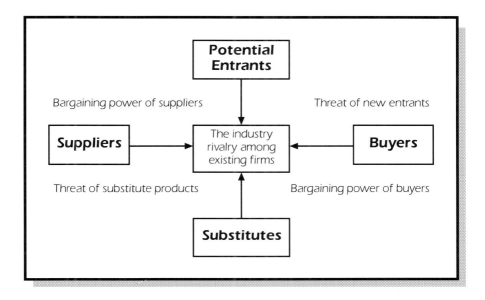

The planning process described in this book sets out a methodology for seeking and highlighting the critical factors in this complex and ever changing scene described by Porter. An industry (or market) operates within an overall environment. If a global industry is under consideration then clearly the environment is the overall social, political and economic scene. Porter's model can be developed to show the elements of a marketing environment that impact upon a specific market. The model shows other elements beyond social, political and economic factors. These are legal, technological and regulatory forces. In different circumstances other external factors can impact on a given market, as shown in the following model of a market and marketing environment:

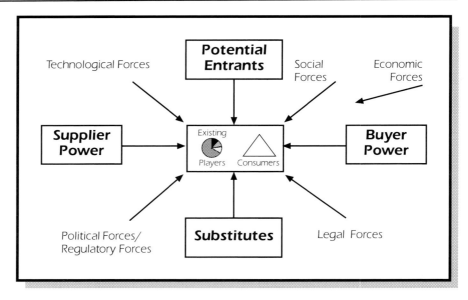

It should be noted that from the point of view of an existing player the majority of the forces that impact upon the market are external to that player. They are therefore beyond his direct control but not necessarily his influence. This depends upon the existing player's position in the market.

It is a fundamental tenet that the marketing planning process seeks out and analyses information on these external forces. These include:

- consumers' needs and wants;
- consumer satisfaction;
- competitive products, services and strategies – direct and from substitutes;
- economic trends;
- social trends;
- political lobbies, regulations;
- current and pending legislation; and
- technological advancements.

Marketing planning is about matching our resources and capabilities to the market situation. These external factors vary in impact from strongly negative (competitive initiatives, for example) to strongly positive (an upturn in the economy, for example). And of course a particular impact can change from positive to negative and vice versa. As an example of how this market structure approach works in practice the following diagram shows a model of the European market for 35mm cameras from the perspective of a domestic manufacturer. This is a large, complex, fast-developing market.

Although the first 35mm camera in the world – the Leica UR – was made in Germany by Oscar Barnack in 1912, the market is now dominated by Japanese manufacturers including Nikon, Canon, Minolta and Pentax. Although Leica and Contax, the early market and technological leaders survive, they occupy high-priced niche positions in the market.

The 35mm single lens reflex (SLR) became increasingly popular during the 1960s and 1970s, with advanced automatic features being added at breakneck pace, as Japanese brands tried to out-do one another. By the mid to late 1980s, consumers had tired of the technology and the most popular 35mm cameras are now automatic rangefinder type – 'point and shoot'. The latest developments include cheap plastic disposable models which still yield more than acceptable results for the average tourist.

A wide range of technological, social, environmental, financial and political factors impact upon this frenzied market. A model of this market using Porter's framework is shown in the next diagram.[2]

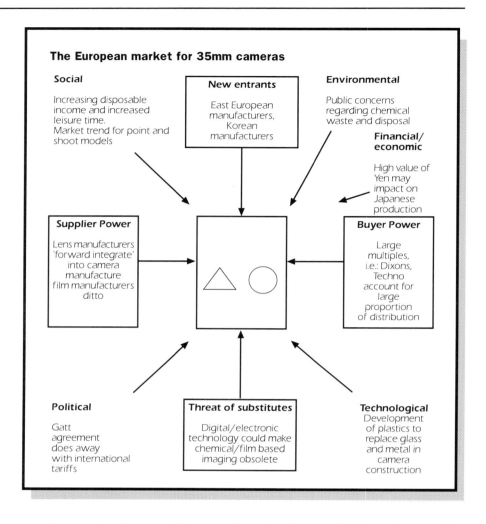

As previously stated this complex situation can be brought to order using relatively simple techniques. A SWOT (strengths, weaknesses, opportunities and threats) analysis for our fictitious European manufacturer could look like the next figure. Note that some factors can be treated as positive (an opportunity) or as negative (a threat) depending on the perspective. In this example we have chosen an opportunistic approach.

Strengths	Weaknesses
• R&D and manufacturing facilities with spare capacity • Established European distribution network • Technical competence in plastics • Financial resources to fund R&D	• Manufacturing costs in German factory 15% higher than in UK • Major competitors have better economies of scale due to very high volume • Japanese manufacturers lead in electronics
Opportunities	**Threats**
• European brand name well known • European market growing rapidly • Japanese products increasing in price by over 12 per cent due to currency fluctuations • Large multiple retailers looking for exclusive supply • Theme park owners seek credible European 'green' supplier	• Japanese brands have market leading 'high tech' image • Korean and Chinese manufacturers entering the market in low price positions • Green lobby could encourage alternative technology • GATT agreement could open door to new low cost entrants • Digital imaging could overtake film based photography

This is one example of how simple analytical techniques in marketing planning can turn chaos into order and significantly help to identify the real issues facing a business. You will probably find that in the early stages of developing your plan, you will be short of factual information. This is quite normal. You will need to develop an approach to help your marketing audit that is increasing the quality and quantity of information about your target markets. There are probably more sources of information than you imagine.

The following list gives some examples:

- trade associates
- business school libraries
- commercial information services
- multi-user marketing research
- bespoke marketing research
- competitive press releases

- competitive annual reports
- customers' annual reports (in business to business markets)
- EC journals and publications
- trade press
- business press
- exhibitions
- government publications
- DTI reports

There is no substitute for a constant flow of good quality information. This will significantly improve your chances of success by raising the standards of your core analyses on which you will base your strategy recommendations and subsequent marketing programmes.

After you have completed your marketing audit and analysis the next step in developing your marketing plan is to develop a strategy. Earlier we discussed the misuse of the term marketing. Strategy is also a term which although used a lot means different things to different people. The dictionary definition of strategy is 'large scale plan or method for winning a war, battle of wits, contest or game'. In a military sense however, strategy literally means deciding on the ground on which you want to fight.

The marketing concept is very much about free trade, market forces and offering the consumer a choice. What is often overlooked is that manufacturers and service providers also have a choice. In this case, who to serve, where and with what products or services and at what price, image and positioning.

The ground on which a marketer must choose to fight can be defined as:

- Segmenting
- Targeting
- Positioning

This determination of marketing strategy cannot be undertaken without a thorough understanding of the marketplace – the marketing analyses described in this workbook – and adequate marketing intelligence.

Put into a marketing context, strategy can be defined as:

the art of allocating and organising our resources in such a way that imposes on the competition the time, place and conditions for competing that match our strengths.

In the research paper quoted earlier (Doyle *et al.*), a marketing director of a British consumer durable goods company was quoted:

> We have not broken the customers down. We have always held the opinion that the market is wide . . . and the product has wide appeal, therefore why break the market down at all.

And so what is wrong with this approach, why segment the market?

The answer to this question can be found in the following quote from Philip Kotler:

> No company can operate in every market and satisfy every need. Nor can it even do a good job within one broad market. Even mighty IBM cannot offer the best customer solution for every computer need. Companies do best when they define their target markets carefully. They do best when they prepare a tailored marketing programme for each target market.

As an example, think of Ford cars in the UK. Traditionally Ford dominated the volume middle ground of the market with *Anglia* and *Cortina* replaced by *Escort* and *Sierra*. When they entered the hatchback market with the *Fiesta* they enjoyed success. However, they have singularly failed to win market share or achieve the price levels of BMW and Mercedes in the executive car class. Their *Granada* range apparently has not met customers' needs and wants as well as the *Escort* and now the *Mondeo* ranges. Ford's ultimate and expensive solution was to buy Jaguar for a price generally regarded to be above its real worth.

We segment markets for many reasons:

- to achieve a differential advantage over existing or new competitors;
- to gain a sustainable share of a sub-market that may not be possible in the total market;
- to avoid weaknesses;
- to match our strengths (internal) to customer needs (external)

This approach leads to:

- a deeper understanding of market needs and wants
- focus for the business
- clear objectives
- defined product and service requirements
- manageable distribution requirements

Segmenting and targeting go hand-in-hand. Positioning is the communication of the determined target market strategy. These crucial strategic issues of marketing are explored well in this workbook's strategy section.

Finally, marketing planning must always result in a detailed set of actions which implement the recommended marketing strategy and which aim to satisfy the targeted customers. These actions manifest themselves in the marketing mix: the determination of product portfolios, branding policies, pricing and payment issues, distribution channels, promotional campaigns and service levels.

These marketing programmes must be specific, clear, achievable and cost-effective. They must reflect the needs of the specified strategy, customers' expectations, competitive activity and market trends. Above all, they must be managed. Line managers have to accept responsibility for ensuring that the programmes are implemented in the business, distributors and in the marketplace. Control mechanisms need to be in place to monitor the progress of the marketing plan and its marketing programmes. The final part of this workbook examines in detail the requirements for determining an effective set of marketing programmes and for monitoring their worth.

There is no doubt as to the importance of marketing in today's business environment. Effective marketing planning is a core element of successful marketing management.

John Bradley, JCB Sales

Notes

1. Doyle, P., Saunders, J. and Wong, V. (1986) 'A Comparative Study of Japanese Marketing Strategies in the British Market', *Journal of International Business Studies*, Vol. 17, No 1.
2. Porter, M.E. (1980) *Competitive Strategy: Techniques for Analyzing Industries and Competitors*, New York: Free Press.

Preface

Marketing Planning: The Rationale

Any business is an evolving organisation: a collection of diverse units, talents and cultures in often fast-changing marketplaces. External pressures affect trading. Corporate goals frequently demand more sales and higher profits. Marketing planning is a process conducted annually in many businesses in order to prioritise target markets, determine marketing programmes and to instil a clear sense of direction for the organisation. In this context, knowing the core issues to address and having a rigorous approach are of growing importance.

This workbook has been prepared to lead managers through the marketing planning process: from the required marketing analyses, into the development of strategies, and finally to the marketing programmes necessary to implement these strategies and take account of the core findings from the analyses.

Each stage of the marketing planning process is discussed, with explanation, guidance, step-by-step instructions and examples. Grids and charts have been produced for simple, quick, self-completion. The marketing plan *document* finally produced will be concise, punchy and totally relevant to the organisation's moves over the next three years and beyond.

The Marketing Planning Workbook is in five sections:

- *Perspective*: an introduction to the marketing planning process.
- *Core Analyses*: existing business, market trends and the marketing environment, capabilities, customers, competitors, product/service portfolio.
- *Analyses into Strategy Recommendations*: mission statement, target markets, differential advantage/basis for competing, brand positioning, marketing objectives.
- *Implementation Programmes*: the marketing mix, responsibilities, budgets, schedules, on-going work, monitoring progress of the marketing plan.
- *The Marketing Plan Document*: requirements and outline structure.

Useful references and additional readings are included.

Marketing planning is essential if a company is to maximise its potential opportunities and internal resources, take advantage of competitors' positions and have a clear sense of direction across the business. The process described in this workbook has been tried and tested in a diversity of international and national organisations covering financial services and retailing, pharmaceuticals and chemicals, construction and engineering, and even in Government agencies.

The Marketing Planning Workbook hinges on the *ASP* principle:

(A) sound marketing Analyses to provide comprehensive and up-to-date marketing intelligence;

(S) a pause to refine marketing Strategy taking account of revised analyses;

(P) the determination of detailed marketing Programmes which incorporate the latest marketing intelligence and implement the determined target market strategies.

Marketing planning is not the sole domain of the corporate marketing director, a business unit or the business development team. It is a *process* or philosophy which endeavours to raise awareness of the marketplace and customer needs, to produce tight strategies and the means for their successful implementation. It is important to involve the *right* personnel in marketing planning, fully orientated and positively motivated. The issues surrounding managing planning initiatives are addressed in the penultimate chapter of this workbook.

By following the stages described in *The Marketing Planning Workbook*, businesses will find they are able to identify the most beneficial target markets and maximise any competitive advantages. The organisation's sales and marketing programmes will make the most of the company's strengths and resources, will minimise weaknesses and help the business to tackle impending threats with confidence. Above all, the resulting marketing programmes will be detailed, actionable and totally geared to satisfying customers and to improving the business's performance.

The Marketing Planning Workbook **must be tackled chapter by chapter and in sequence.**

Good luck with your marketing planning.

Sally Dibb & Lyndon Simkin

About the Authors

In 1991 Sally Dibb and Lyndon Simkin joined with US colleagues Bill Pride and O.C. Ferrell to produce *Marketing: Concepts and Strategies* (published by Houghton Mifflin). Now in its second edition this text dominates the business school market in the UK, Eire, Benelux and much of Scandinavia. To coincide with the second edition of this text, Sally and Lyndon published *The Marketing Casebook: Cases and Concepts*, through Routledge in 1994. This innovative package created new ground by combining 15 real company cases with theory notes, glossary and readings to create a self-learn text.

Married with three children – Becky, James and baby Abby – Sally and Lyndon have been lecturing to MBAs and undergraduates at the University of Warwick Business School since the mid-1980s.

Sally has a BSc (management science) and MSc (industrial marketing) from UMIST in Manchester and a PhD (consumer marketing modelling) from Warwick. Lyndon was once an economic geographer (BA, Leicester) before switching to marketing (PhD) at the University of Bradford's Management Centre. Their current publications are in the areas of marketing modelling, market segmentation, marketing planning, marketing communications and services marketing. Consultancy is diverse, ranging from car parts, diggers, chemicals, cameras, IT to burgers and catalogue retailing; in the UK, Europe and beyond! Some of these experiences are touched upon in this workbook.

Graduating in engineering, John Bradley toured the world with JCB Sales before becoming Corporate Marketing Director. Under John, JCB's marketing prowess blossomed, with some of the most professional promotional campaigns, branding and successful product launches seen in the construction equipment industry. Helped by stints at INSEAD and the London Business School, John mixes a shrewd understanding of strategic marketing concepts with a realistic grasp of practical tactical applications. In 1995 John became general manager for JCB's £70 million parts and attachments business. Sally and Lyndon have worked with John at JCB for the past six years, during which period many of the 'tricks' discussed in this workbook were developed and fine-tuned.

If you have any queries, please contact Sally and Lyndon by fax on

01926 851561 or by telephone at the University of Warwick on 01203 523523.

Readers finding the format of this workbook to their liking should note that a sister title is available, *The Market Segmentation Workbook*, London: Routledge, 1996.

Acknowledgements

We wish to thank several retail and services organisations whose personnel have assisted in the development of ideas and tools utilised herein. In addition, we express our gratitude to three businesses: ICI, Zeneca and DRA. Without the co-operation of these companies this workbook would not have been possible. Specifically:

John Greaves, *Zeneca*
Sam Hay, *ICI Market Focus Bureau*
David A. Smith, *DRA CIS*
Jayne Ackroyd, *DRA*
Anita Hunt, Lynne Stainthorpe *Tioxide UK*
Peter Jackson, *Adsearch London*

Section I

Perspective

Section I outlines the characteristics of marketing planning, the role which it plays in an organisation and the process required to produce sound, realistic and effective plans.

- Marketing planning defined
- The importance of marketing planning
- The marketing planning process

1

Marketing Planning

1.1 Introduction

Marketing planning is an approach adopted by many successful, market-focused businesses. While it is by no means a new tool, the degree of objectivity and thoroughness with which it is applied varies considerably. This book presents a straightforward format for conducting comprehensive marketing analyses, making the most of the resulting marketing intelligence to determine marketing strategies, and for ensuring detailed, actionable marketing programmes are put in place which implement the recommended strategies: the ultimate objective of a marketing planning initiative. In order to put the step-by-step guidance into context, the book begins with a brief overview of the marketing planning process and the benefits which it offers.

1.2 Definitions

The *Marketing Concept* holds that the key to achieving organisational goals lies in determining the needs and wants of target markets, and delivering the desired 'satisfaction' more effectively and efficiently than competitors.

Marketing Planning is a systematic process involving assessing marketing opportunities and resources, determining marketing objectives, and developing a plan for implementation and control.

The *Marketing Plan* is the written document or blueprint for implementing and controlling an organisation's marketing activities related to a particular marketing strategy.

A company's marketing *Opportunity* is an attractive arena for company marketing action in which the company would enjoy a competitive advantage.

1.3 Why Bother with Marketing Planning?

Formal marketing planning is not a whim of text books or a few marketing directors. It is a recognised, popular approach in many successful, customer-orientated organisations. From ICI, Shell, to Electrolux or Heineken, marketing planning keeps companies in-tune with trends in the marketplace, abreast of customer needs, and aware of the competition. Planning helps ensure that resources are utilised effectively, and that businesses are ready to respond to the unexpected.

- Marketing planning hinges on core analyses of trends, customers, competition and capabilities.
- Marketing planning develops strategies which target the most lucrative customers.
- The strategies which planning generates should concentrate on the organisation's real and perceived advantages in its markets.
- Action programmes – marketing mixes – help to ensure the implementation of the strategies which have been developed.
- Resources are concentrated on achieving the programmes which are developed.

Some companies operate 3- or 5-yearly planning cycles; some every six months. Most common perhaps is an annual revision with a 3-year focus. In this way, the marketing plan includes detailed recommendations for the next 2 years, with extrapolations for the third year. The detailed analyses and plans are then updated annually.

Put simply, marketing planning is all about:

- hitting the *best* customer targets;
- winning new customers;
- expanding markets;
- beating the competition;
- keeping abreast of market developments;
- maximising returns;
- using resources to best advantage;
- minimising threats; and
- identifying company strengths or weaknesses.

Without marketing planning, it is more difficult to guide research and development (R&D) and new product development (NPD); set required standards for suppliers; guide the sales force in terms of what to emphasise, to whom, and what/whom to avoid; set realistic, achievable sales targets; avoid competitor actions or changes in the marketplace. Above all, businesses which fail to incorporate marketing planning into their marketing activities may therefore not be in a position to develop a sustainable competitive edge in their markets.

1.4 The Marketing Planning Approach

There is a logical and straightforward approach to marketing planning:

a) consideration of the organisation's mission statement;

b) analysis of markets and the trading environment;

c) determination of core target markets;

d) identification of differential advantage(s);

e) statement of goals and desired product/service positioning; and

f) development of marketing programmes and budgets to implement plans.

The organisation's mission statement helps provide an overall sense of direction and puts the marketing planning into context. The analysis of the marketing environment, target markets and existing and new competitors (direct and indirect) creates a firm foundation for decision-making. Without an understanding of customer segments, trends and competitors, the marketing programme may not have a clear and appropriate sense of direction.

The marketer must determine a basis for competing or a competitive edge in each of the targeted market segments. The selection of target markets and the determination of a differential advantage must take into account the organisation's capabilities, and its strengths and weaknesses. The determined strategy should also relate to the organisation's mission statement or sense of purpose.

To implement the planned strategy, a marketing programme must be formulated which – through the elements of the marketing mix – takes the product, service or expertise to the targeted customers in the most beneficial and clear manner.

The costs associated with implementing this marketing programme must be calculated and justified. Accurate sales forecasts should be developed which identify the likely returns.

1.5 The Process

This book organises marketing planning into three stages: Analysis, Strategy, and Programmes (see Figure 1.1). These stages incorporate all aspects of the marketing planning approach described above. The analysis stage involves the collection and organisation of information about markets and the trading environment. The strategy stage encompasses the determination of core target markets, identification of differential advantages and decisions about positioning. Lastly, the programmes stage involves the construction of detailed marketing mixes and implementation actions.

Figure 1.1   The ASP Approach to Marketing Planning

1. Analysis

- Analysis of market opportunities and trends
- Analysis of the marketing environment and market trends
- Analysis of the organisation's Strengths, Weaknesses, Opportunities and Threats - SWOT
- Analysis of customers' needs and perceptions; market segmentation and brand positioning
- Analysis of competition and competitors' strategies

2. Strategy decisions

- Determination of core target markets
- Basis for competing/differential advantage
- Desired product positioning
- Marketing objectives/sales targets

3. Programmes for implementation

- Specification of plans for marketing mix programmes:
  - Products
  - Promotion
  - Place: distribution/marketing channels
  - Pricing/payment terms
  - People/service levels
- Specification of tasks, responsibilities, timing, costs and budgets
- On-going work/additional development
- Monitoring progress/measuring effectiveness of the plan

Source: Adapted from Sally Dibb and Lyndon Simkin (1994)
The Marketing Casebook: Cases and Concepts, London: Routledge.

1.6 The Marketing Plan Document

The final task of marketing planning is to summarise the salient findings from the marketing analyses, the strategic recommendations and the required marketing programmes in a short report: the written marketing plan. This document needs to be concise, yet complete in terms of presenting a summary of the marketplace and the business's position, explaining thoroughly the recommended strategy and containing the detail of the required marketing mix actions. For many managers, the written plan will be all they glean from the marketing planning activity. It must, therefore, be informative, to the point, while mapping out a clear set of marketing activities designed to satisfactorily implement the desired target market strategy.

1.7 The Planning Cycle

Marketing planning is an on-going analysis/planning/control process or cycle (see Figure 1.2). Many organisations update their marketing plans annually as new information becomes available. Once incorporated, the key recommendations can then be presented to senior managers within the organisation. Companies which are developing marketing plans for the first time, are usually relieved to find that the workload reduces year-on-year, as updating requires less input. Much of the heartache comes in the initiation of marketing planning!

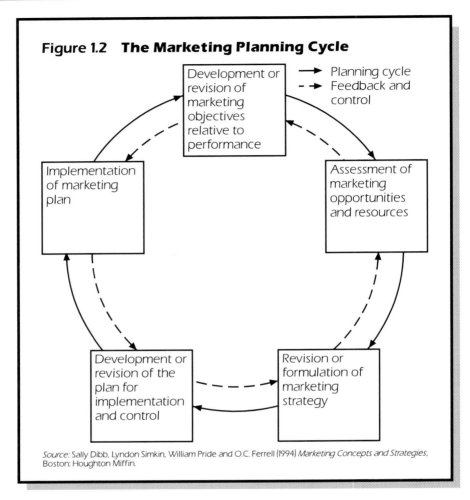

Figure 1.2 The Marketing Planning Cycle

→ Planning cycle
--→ Feedback and control

- Development or revision of marketing objectives relative to performance
- Assessment of marketing opportunities and resources
- Revision or formulation of marketing strategy
- Development or revision of the plan for implementation and control
- Implementation of marketing plan

Source: Sally Dibb, Lyndon Simkin, William Pride and O.C. Ferrell (1994) *Marketing Concepts and Strategies*, Boston: Houghton Miffin.

1.8 Summary

Marketing planning is an effective tool for understanding the mechanics of target markets and for formalising a business's sense of direction. Having completed essential background marketing analyses, the marketing team should be in a position to determine the business's strategic direction: identifying the priority target markets, deciding about the desired brand positioning in each market, establishing where the business benefits from any advantage over competitors and determining the core marketing objectives. Details are provided in the marketing plan document of the specific marketing action programmes required to implement the strategic direction, in the target market(s) identified. These programmes must make the most of identified marketing opportunities with the optimum use of the business's personnel, time and budgets. This book is structured to thoroughly review each of these steps, and commences with an examination of the required marketing analyses.

Section I Checklist

By the end of this *Perspective* section of *The Marketing Planning Workbook* you should have:

- Comprehended the nature of marketing planning
- Understood the importance of the marketing planning process and started to consider its relevance to the business
- Reviewed the marketing planning approach

The Marketing Planning Workbook

Section I
Perspective

Section II
Core Analyses

Section III
Analyses into Strategy

Section IV
Programmes for Implementation

Section V
The Marketing Plan Document

Section II

Core Analyses

The success of marketing planning depends on developing a clear understanding of the marketplace and trends. Core marketing analyses are essential in order to consolidate marketing intelligence, prior to making strategic decisions. Section II outlines the information required which will determine the strategic decisions made. A number of templates are included which can be used to record the findings of the analyses.

- Existing business
- Market trends and the marketing environment
- Strengths, weaknesses, opportunities, threats – SWOT
- Customers' needs, buying processes and influences
- Competition and competitors' strategies
- The balance of the product portfolio and the product life cycle

2

Existing Markets/Sectors

2.1 Introduction

In any business, the marketing planning process must begin with an examination of the current mix of customers and their worth to the organisation. The purpose of this review is to assess the current state of marketing thinking and actions within the organisation, as this is likely to form some of the basis for the newly developed marketing plan.

For most companies the existing view of customer segments and primary sales targets will be based on a mix of common sense and historical information about the market and individual customers. For example, a manufacturer of children's car seats will receive a range of feedback from consumers who buy their products. This gives the company an intuitive feel of customer reaction to and perception of its products. The company will be able to combine this information with sales figures, to build up a wider picture of the market.

Inevitably businesses may find there are gaps in their information, or that there is a need to update their perceptions. This is important because in most organisations, 'historical perceptions' of the relative importance of different groups of customers will impact on targeting and sales forecasting policy. With the pace of change of customer needs and the volatility of markets in terms of competition and market trends, there is always a need to re-examine targets.

This chapter presents a straightforward approach for analysing the importance to the business of existing customer groups and markets. This analysis helps get marketing planning underway by assisting businesses to re-appraise their market priorities.

2.2 Approaches to the Analysis

There are four key stages for companies wishing to re-examine their existing customer base, priorities, and segments. These stages help the business to identify the importance of different markets and customer groups.

1. State how customers are broken down currently into sub-groups or segments by the business. For example, in business to business or industrial markets, by customers' industry sector; their customer type;

their purchasing patterns (seasonal, regular, etc); the types of products purchased; territory, location or whatever. In consumer markets, the business may have determined segments by sales patterns, social class, age, sex, lifestyle, buying patterns, retail orientation, etc. No matter what criteria are used it is helpful to consider whether such categorisations are commonplace within the industry

2. For each existing segment or identified group of customers, summarise the product, dealer, sales and marketing needs which the business must be able to satisfy.

These needs, sometimes referred to as Key Customer Values (KCVs), represent the principal sales, product and marketing aspects valued or demanded by customers.

Steps 1 and 2 can be summarised simply. Figure 2.1 shows these steps using the 35mm camera market as an example.

Figure 2.1 Summary of Existing Target Market Segments

Example: 35mm camera market

Customer Group or Market Segment	These Customers' Key Needs (KCVs)	Adopted Descriptions Used by the Business to Describe Target Market Segment
1 *Professionals*	*Reliability Performance*	*Pros*
2 *Advanced Amateurs*	*Feature level Performance*	*Buffs*
3 *Amateurs*	*Convenience Feature level*	*Amateurs*
4 *Occasional Users*	*Simplicity*	*Weekenders*
5		
6		

- Rank segments in column 1 in order of importance to the business
- For each segment, rank the KCVs listed in column 2
- Define KCV term if required so as to avoid ambiguity

For example, some car manufacturers segment their markets in terms of car engine size. These manufacturers know that customer needs (KCVs) for the resulting categories of vehicle are different. The typical potential buyer of the 'small' car, may place much more importance on economy and fuel efficiency, than the purchaser of a car from the 'large executive' category, who might be much more concerned about the luxury of the interior.

Figure 2.2 Importance of Current Markets, Last 10 Years

Rank Order of Markets by Year (Current year = t)										
Segment	t-9	t-8	t-7	t-6	t-5	t-4	t-3	t-2	t-1	t
1										
2										
3										
4										
5										
6										
7										
8										

Reasons for Major Changes

- Rank each market's importance over the years. Importance may be in terms of sales volumes, market share, profitability or contribution
- Explain any major changes in rank position year on year

3. Many business find that the composition of these markets has changed over time, and that the importance of each market to the business has altered. Tabulate for the past ten years the rank order of importance of these markets to the business, adding explanatory footnotes where the running order alters significantly (e.g. if a market ranked 2 in 1987 is only ranked 9 in 1996). See Figure 2.2.

4. Summarising these year on year moves should have raised a number of concerns and questions. Why is so much importance placed on market 'X'? Why is the sales force still devoting so much resource to market 'Y'? What about market 'A' – suddenly it seems more important? Is it? For example, an agricultural equipment manufacturer which historically had a presence in many countries discovered that the importance of one South East Asian market had declined dramatically. Despite this decline, the company had continued, without questioning why, to commit a high level of marketing resource to the area.

This example provides a pertinent lead into the final stage of this analysis, which involves examining the recent history of the business to evaluate the financial worth of each market – and major individual customers – to the business.

A common and relatively simple approach is to examine sales and contribution (the financial value to the company) of each market, using an ABC Pareto Analysis. The next two sections explain the mechanics of the analysis for different markets (segment or territories) and individual customer accounts.

2.3 The ABC Sales: Contribution Analysis

2.3.1 For Market Segments or Territories

The ABC Sales: Contribution Analysis can be conducted at either Product or Product Mix level. Businesses must select the level which seems appropriate to their situation. For example, an importer of fashion wear may choose to evaluate the contribution for different ranges of clothes, while a truck manufacturer might focus on individual models.

Data required
Start by listing out, market by market, current sales in either volume or turnover. Turnover (e.g. £s or $s) is more common.

Next, for each market (segment or territory), list the current levels of financial contribution (sales revenue minus all variable costs).

Plot graph

On a standard, two dimensional (X-axis and Y-axis) graph, plot out sales and contributions. Log scales may be appropriate, subject to data ranges, in order to condense the plot if the range of data is great. Normally, however, a straightforward plot of the raw numbers should suffice.

- Y-axis (vertical): sales.
- X-axis (horizontal): contribution.

Evaluation

In an ideal world, the dots on the graph – each dot represents a market (segment or territory) – would be located at the top right of the graph: high sales and high contribution. In simple terms this equates to 'sell a lot, make a lot': 'A' class markets.

Many businesses find that this is not the case for them. The majority of markets may fall at the bottom left of the graph (low sales and low contribution: 'C' class markets), or may have reasonably high sales, but low contributions ('B' class).

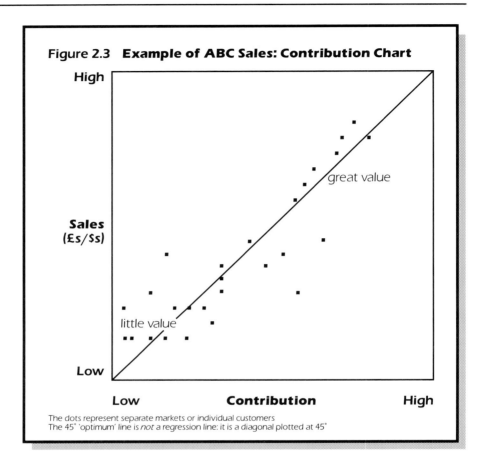

Figure 2.3 **Example of ABC Sales: Contribution Chart**

The dots represent separate markets or individual customers
The 45° 'optimum' line is *not* a regression line: it is a diagonal plotted at 45°

Diagnosis

Figure 2.3 shows an ABC Sales: Contribution chart for a European manufacturer. In general, businesses will find that not all of the plotted markets will be close to the 45-degree diagonal line optimum. There will be a range of outliers which require attention.

A question mark should hang over any market located in the bottom left of the graph: these markets are draining sales and marketing resources, without offering any obvious return to the organisation. However, there may still be good reasons for retaining a presence in these markets and businesses must consider carefully whether there is any benefit in continuing to service these markets. Is a presence needed to protect the business's other products and markets from competitive in-roads? Would other customers worry if the business pulled away from these low-benefit customers? Are there seasonal reasons for this currently poor return? If the answers are 'no', the business may need to consider focusing its marketing effort on a new market (segment or territory). For example, a pharmaceutical retailer may identify a significant proportion of skin-care products which make little contribution to the business. However, customers in the retail outlets, who typically go into the stores to buy a variety of different items, expect to find a full range of such products.

Where concerns are raised, companies must consider what improvements can be made. High volume markets to the upper left of the 45-degree line, with low contributions, would be of tremendous value if contributions were increased by only a few per cent. Similarly, high contribution markets where currently volumes are low (those plotted to the lower right of the 45-degree line) are crucial targets: an even minor increase in sales volumes should be very lucrative to the business.

Clearly such 'movements' and improvements are not always possible. For markets in the bottom left of the graph, harsh decisions may be required, as these markets seem to be of little value to the company.

2.3.2 For Individual Customer Accounts

So far this ABC Sales: Contribution analysis has concentrated on the market (segment or territory) level. The completed analysis may well show a whole market to have relatively little value for the business. In such cases it may be particularly appropriate to move to the second level of analysis, where individual key customer accounts are examined in a similar manner.

Once again, this analysis can be either by Product or Product Mix.

Data required
Begin by listing out, customer by customer, current sales in either volume or turnover. Turnover (e.g. £s or $s) is more common.

Next, for each customer, list the current levels of financial contribution (sales revenues minus all variable costs).

Plot graph
On a standard, two dimensional (X-axis and Y-axis) graph, plot out sales and contributions. Log scales may be required to condense the plot owing to data ranges.

- Y-axis (vertical): sales.
- X-axis (horizontal): contribution.

The final two stages, evaluation and diagnosis, follow the same pattern as described in the previous section. However, in general, companies may find that it is relatively easier to drop customers of little value (those in the bottom left of the graph) than entire segments.

2.3.3 Recording the ABC Sales: Contribution Chart

Figure 2.4 can be used to record the sales and contributions either for all key markets (segments or territories) or for principal customers. The axes should be labelled as appropriate. One approach is to begin by looking at all markets, before making judgements about which represent high and low sales and contribution, then mark the axes accordingly. Next, use the guidelines above to evaluate the attractiveness of the markets or customers plotted.

Figure 2.4 The ABC Sales: Contribution Chart

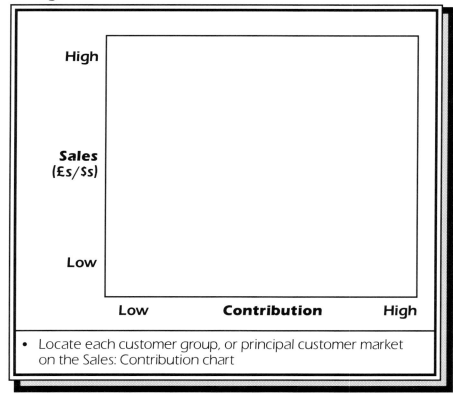

2.4 **Summary**

These straightforward analyses have presented an important overview of the nature of existing customer groups or markets, their key characteristics, their relative importance in recent years to the business, and their current value in terms of sales volume and contribution.

These analyses may demonstrate a need to re-think target market priorities and to keep abreast of a changing marketplace. If the examination of current markets has not prompted modifications to target market strategy and marketing programmes, the outcome from the analyses described in the remainder of Section II probably will encourage changes.

There will, though, be some significant strengths in the existing approach to customer targeting, and therefore to sales and marketing. These background analyses, together with further analyses detailed in the following chapters, will highlight these strengths and help to ensure that this marketing planning exercise builds upon the organisation's current assets.

3

Market Trends and the Marketing Environment

3.1 Introduction

It is always important for businesses to maintain an understanding of the trends in the marketplace, but this is particularly crucial when developing marketing plans. Ultimately the business will wish, through the planning process, to target markets which are likely to offer high volume and value, both currently and in the future. For this reason marketing planning helps organisations identify healthy and declining markets so that resources can be appropriately directed (this point is followed up in Chapter 7). Reviewing market trends, so that an overall picture can be developed, involves the business examining both general trends and marketplace statistics.

For all businesses there are factors over which the company has no direct control, but which do impact upon the company and its trading performance. Issues regarding social pressures, legal, regulatory, political controls, technological changes, economic swings, together with more focused concerns about suppliers and competition. These issues collectively make up *the marketing environment*. This chapter considers the market trends which may impact upon the business and explores the different aspects of the marketing environment.

3.2 Market Trends

A *market* is defined as an aggregate of people or businesses who need products in particular product classes and who have the ability, willingness and authority to purchase such goods. Markets can be broken into segments: each *segment* consists of a group of customers who share similar characteristics resulting in them having relatively similar product needs.

In order to plan and make sound strategic decisions, companies must have an awareness of the numerical trends in the market. For example, a bakery which is considering developing a new range of fresh cream cakes would need to understand the potential demand for the products. In order to forecast the likely demand, the bakery should consider the overall market size and spread, as well as the level of competition. The bakery should then examine the potential financial value to the business of the market. The following list summarises some of the key trends which businesses must consider when undertaking marketing planning:

- Sales: volume
- Sales: financial values
- Profitability
- Market size
- Market shares
- Numbers and sizes of customers
- Numbers of key competitors

Figure 3.1 presents a summary chart for this information. The information for the current year has been filled in using a manufacturer's results from a consumer goods market.

Figure 3.1 **Core Market Trends and Predictions**

Year	Sales Volumes (Units)	Sales (£s/$s) 000's	Profitability (£s/$s) 000's	Market Size	Business's Market Share	Number of Customers	Number of Main Competitors
t-5							
t-4							
t-3							
t-2							
t-1							
current year (t)	11,204	274,498	14.3	98,280 units	11.4%	4,668	5
t+1							
t+2							
t+3							
t+4							

Market:

- Complete as many columns as possible
- Information beyond the current year is based on predictions
- For many markets, the business will not know market shares
- Principal customers: most businesses have an '80:20' split - the bulk of sales (e.g. '80%') comes from a minority of customers (e.g. '20%')
- Principal competitors (direct) indicate the level of market activity and, to a degree, the 'attractiveness' of the market

3.3 The Marketing Environment

> The marketing environment is made up of those external forces that directly or indirectly influence an organisation's acquisitions of inputs and generation of outputs.

In other words, these forces are aspects of the trading environment over which the business has very little direct control, but are elements which will tangibly affect the way in which the organisation can do business and will perform.

Most companies have at least some understanding of their trading environment, although this information may be poorly communicated amongst members of the organisation. This analysis makes sure information is pooled and incorporated within the development of marketing strategy.

To monitor changes in the marketing environment, marketers must undertake a continual process of scanning and analysis. Some companies handle this using individual marketing managers or committees whose function is to collect and collate data related to trends in the market and aspects of the marketing environment. For example, in one manufacturing organisation, a small committee meets regularly to identify pertinent marketing environment issues. Updates are then posted on a staff notice board which is openly accessible.

Environmental Scanning is the process of tracking information from observation, secondary sources (particularly the trade press and government reports), databases, information services and marketing research.

The marketing environment generally is broken into two key sections, termed the *macro* marketing environment and the *micro* marketing environment.

3.3.1 The Macro Environment

The main elements of the macro environment are outlined below.

Legal forces

Many laws influence marketing activities; for example, UK companies must conform with pro-competitive legislation and consumer protection legislation. The EU and NAFTA are big influences in this context.

Regulatory forces

Interpretation of laws is important, but so is an understanding of the enforcement by the various government ministries and local government departments, plus the non-government regulatory bodies, such as GATT or trade and professional associations.

Political forces

Many marketers view the actions of government as beyond influence, while others successfully lobby and influence the policy making and legislating bodies of central and local governments. It is therefore important also to understand the likely impact of other people's lobbying activities. Likely political policy changes must be monitored.

Societal forces (culture)

These are the dynamics and workings of society: groups and individuals often ignore the activities of companies and marketers until they infringe on their lifestyles and choices. Perhaps the most significant current example is the Green movement with consumer pressure on companies to produce products which are less harmful to the earth's environment, with less waste, and which are produced in a more ecologically sensitive manner. Another recent trend has been the public's condemnation of the transport of live animals. Some airlines and shipping companies have bowed to public pressure by refusing to engage in these activities.

Technological forces

These refer to the technological expertise with which to accomplish tasks and goals. Technology is quickly evolving and changing, affecting how people satisfy their needs and lead their lives. Technology is changing in production, distribution, communications and selling, affecting the products marketers can bring to the marketplace and how they are presented to customers. For example, the computer industry has been significantly affected by the highly successful development of Windows-based applications.

Economic conditions

General economic conditions – recession or boom – will impact on any market, as will customer demand and spending behaviour. These are important considerations for any marketer, particularly as such conditions can be volatile, prone to dramatic changes, patterns and fashions. The building industry is particularly hard-hit by the effects of economic recession. Even once there is an economic upturn, it can take a long time for confidence to return.

3.3.2 The Micro Environment

The elements of the micro marketing environment are aspects for which the impacts are company/organisation specific rather than market specific. The degree of control which the business has over these factors is usually small. The key items to consider for the micro environment are listed below.

Direct and substitute competition

The nature and degree of competition in a product area from similar products are important. Model proliferation is a competitive weapon used by major players such as Toshiba, IBM or Canon. In addition, the possibility of competition from substitute products must be considered. Japanese developed tunnelling robotic moles are a threat to traditional JCB excavators. In general, it is important to consider the degree to which the competitive situation is stable. For example, the emergence of a number of new competitors may radically alter the existing status quo.

Supplier influence/power

Most companies prefer independence and the opportunity to exert control over their suppliers. Control is not always possible: suppliers, particularly in situations where there are very few or if the products supplied are innovative or unique, can become uncomfortably strong. Co-operation can reduce the risks posed by such suppliers, so companies may seek to develop long-term relationships. In such cases, care must be taken to avoid complacency and to question the stability of the supplier relationship.

The company's resource base

The resource base in terms of supplies and materials, finances, people, time and goodwill is generally in the control of the business itself. There are occasions, though, when trends in the marketplace and in the marketing environment act to strengthen or weaken the resource base. For example new industry-wide working practices, legislation, altered banking policies, customer pressures and demands, all alter the resource base. Activities which can affect the availability of resources must be carefully monitored.

Customers' buying power

Customers' requirements and perceptions must constantly be monitored, especially as these factors can be susceptible to underlying trends in the market which increase or reduce customer buying power (see Chapter 5). For example, a proliferation of companies offering keenly priced motor insurance has increased the power of customers, who can buy their insurance more easily and cheaply than before. The result of such changes will have significant impact on a business's performance and so the likelihood of such changes in buying power must be checked.

No matter what the company or market, there are always elements of the marketing environment which directly impact on the competence of a company's performance and its ability to trade in a market. It is therefore vital that a careful monitoring programme is instigated.

3.3.3 Monitoring the Marketing Environment

In any situation not all aspects of the macro or micro marketing environment will be causing debate. But some will, and perhaps others should! Often managers think about market trends and developments which may affect their organisation's business, but they fail to articulate these concerns. In a marketing planning programme, they must be discussed, as market trends will inevitably impact on the choice of which markets to target, on where products and brands should be positioned in the marketplace, and how – the marketing mix.

Marketing environment trends likely to affect the business need to be summarised (see Figure 3.2). This chart is a simple statement of issues thought likely to be important. Once complete, and merged with similar charts from colleagues' analyses, the leading issues can be prioritised and examined further. Individual managers will need to be allocated to look into separate issues and trends.

Figure 3.2 The Marketing Environment Issues

Summary of Core Issues

Macro Environment
(legal, regulatory and political, societal, technological, economic)

Micro Environment
(direct and substitute competition, new entrants, supplier influence, customer buying power)

Principal Implications to the Business of These Issues

- Consider the wide range of potentially relevant aspects
- Be prudent and objective - list only important concerns
- List the most pressing/crucial issues first
- Have evidence to support these assertions
- Have facts with sources with which to defend statements

3.4 Summary

The analyses presented in this chapter have examined the statistical trends in the core markets as well as the general marketing environment issues likely to have some impact on the business, its suppliers, competitors and customers. While the business may have little direct influence over these factors, they nevertheless must be tackled if the business is to perform as desired.

The statistical trends are an important reflection of the business's performance, its stature in its markets and its likely potential: sales volume/value, market size/share, profitability, number and size of leading customers and the number of key competitors. The wider marketing environment includes legal, regulatory, political, societal, technological and economic macro forces, plus the micro concerns of direct competition, substitutes, supplier influence and customer buying power. To avoid damaging surprises and to maximise opportunities, these issues must be monitored and evaluated.

4

SWOT Analysis: Strengths, Weaknesses, Opportunities and Threats

4.1 Introduction

The *SWOT* (sometimes referred to as *TOWS*) analysis is one of the most commonly implemented analyses in marketing, as well as in other disciplines such as Total Quality Management (TQM). The aim of this analysis is to summarise the business's strengths and weaknesses in relation to the competition and highlight external factors which are impacting upon the market's performance.

A simple format for presentation is illustrated in Figure 4.1: strengths, weaknesses, opportunities and threats. Strengths and weaknesses are issues *internal* to an organisation, while opportunities and threats relate to *external* aspects of the marketplace (many of which stem from an analysis of the marketing environment). Marketing planning is littered with ill-thought out and irrelevant SWOT analyses. In some respects this is the price paid for the simplicity of the analysis. It is therefore important that the SWOT is not merely a collection of managers' hunches. It must be based on objective facts and on marketing research findings. The SWOT analysis should:

a) focus on the most crucial 'hot' issues, and

b) be relative to the strongest competitors in a particular market.

The SWOT gives a clear picture of the business's situation and where action is required to maximise opportunities and minimise threats and weaknesses.

A SWOT analysis can be used in a number of different ways by businesses. Many organisations undertake the analysis for each of the markets in which they operate. Some businesses also find it helpful to produce SWOT grids for each leading competitor. This helps reveal the companies' relative strengths and weaknesses and ability to face the identified threats and opportunities. This chapter reviews the SWOT analysis and provides instructions for preparing effective, tightly focused analyses.

Figure 4.1 **The SWOT Grid**

Internal factors	*Strengths*	*Weaknesses*
External factors	*Opportunities*	*Threats*

4.2 Effective SWOT Analysis

The SWOT is one of simplest and most widely used of marketing analyses. An effective SWOT should provide a succinct, interesting and readable summary of the state of the business and the external factors and trends impacting upon it. The reader should be left with little doubt about the state of the market, the business's orientation towards it and within it. In order to achieve this the information contained within the SWOT should be comprehensive, relevant and specific. A useful test of an effective SWOT is whether the analysis has clear implications for the business's future sense of direction.

Unfortunately, despite the many benefits which SWOT analysis offers, all too often the inherent simplicity of the technique is also its undoing and can lead to output which is vague, confused, irrelevant and lacking direction. The following pointers should be followed to avoid some of these pitfalls.

- Make the SWOT as focused as possible. For example, the business may decide to develop the analysis at the level of the customer segment, geographic territory or even the product. Once a decision about the focus has been reached, only incorporate information which is directly relevant.

- Strengths and Weaknesses must reflect the position of the business in relation to competing organisations. A strength is only a strength if the business is better at this aspect of its offering than competitors.
- Record items as succinctly and carefully as possible. Interpretation (like beauty) is usually in the eye of the beholder! Two managers interpreting the same, loosely worded SWOT may generate different interpretations.

4.3 Internal Environment Issues: Strengths and Weaknesses

A SWOT analysis can deal with any aspect of the internal environment which is perceived as relevant by managers and customers. When considering the Strengths and Weaknesses, the following areas will usually be considered:

Marketing
Products
Pricing
Promotion
Marketing Information/Intelligence
Resources
Service/People
Distribution/Distributors
Branding and Positioning

For example, a fast food retailer which has commissioned marketing research to review the effectiveness of its current advertising campaign may decide, based on the research findings, that its promotional activities are a strength.

Engineering and product development
Often of peripheral importance, however with new Total Quality Management initiatives, the relationship between engineering/production and marketing may be becoming more formalised. Companies which enjoy the benefits of good internal relationships between marketing and engineering may believe that an excellent record in new product development which has been generated should be recorded as a strength.

Operations
Production/Engineering
Sales and Marketing
Processing Orders/Transactions
Economies of Scale

A packaging company which is unable to generate sufficient orders to achieve scale economies may list this as a weakness, particularly if customers complain about their products being overpriced.

People
R&D
Distributors
Marketing
Sales
After Sales/Service
Processing/Customer Service

This category covers a wide range of people related issues, including skills; wages/benefits; training and development; motivation; conditions; staff turnover. The role of people is central to the successful implementation of a customer focused marketing philosophy and the marketing strategy in businesses of all kinds.

Management
Sensitive and often a contentious area, but weaknesses here may mean that management structures and philosophies need altering to facilitate the successful implementation of a marketing strategy. For example, the need for strategic alliances, partnerships and mergers may be indicated, or a revised management hierarchy.

Company resources
This aspect will impact upon any actions which arise out of the SWOT analysis. People and financial resources must be considered.

4.4 External Environment Issues: Threats and Opportunities

The external environment issues relate strongly to the marketing environment (see Chapter 3 above). The core features to consider include:

- Social/Cultural
- Regulatory/Legal/Political
- Technological
- Economic Conditions
- Competition:
  Global players
  International versus national versus local ability
  Intensity of rivalry
  Threat of entry
  Pressure from substitutions
  Market's customer needs
  Bargaining power of buyers, distributors, suppliers

From a thorough SWOT analysis, an organisation can glean initial insights into distinctive competencies and differential advantage over rivals; customer needs (to a degree, and often only with an internal, company-personnel view); product portfolio requirements; competitive positioning; assumptions on which strategic decisions will be based; the match of the company's status with stated corporate goals; as well as the more obvious remarks concerning marketing opportunities and threats, company strengths and weaknesses.

4.5 To Conduct the SWOT

For each segment or market under review, list the most important issues in each of the four elements of the SWOT grid – Strengths, Weaknesses, Opportunities and Threats. See Figure 4.2.

In each of the four sections of the SWOT, ensure that the points listed are in ranked order of importance: put the most important threat first, and so on. There is no point listing dozens of issues: emphasise only those points of most impact on the business. Be objective: can the assertions be backed up with evidence (quotations, letters, trade statistics, press reports, government publications, sales force feedback, customer comments)?

Do not lose sight of the fact that the points listed should be taking account of the business's position versus its strongest rivals.

Figure 4.2 **The SWOT Analysis in Planning**

Strengths	Weaknesses
Opportunities	**Threats**

- Rank (list) points in order of importance
- Only include key points/issues
- Have evidence to support these points
- Strengths and Weaknesses should be relative to main competitors
- Strengths and Weaknesses are *internal* issues
- Opportunities and Threats are *external* competitive and marketing environment issues

What are the core implications from these issues?

4.5 **Summary**

This chapter has reviewed the development of the SWOT analysis. This simple approach allows companies to review the opportunities present in the marketplace and weigh up their capabilities for pursuing them. An appreciation of the threats that may impact on the business's position can also be achieved. Adopting a customer-focused view of the business's strengths and weaknesses helps to ensure realistic decisions are made about where to direct resources, helping the business to make the best of available opportunities.

5

Customer Needs (KCVs), Expectations and Buying Processes – Now and in the Future

5.1 Introduction

Many companies find that they must cater for the needs of a wide range of different customer types. By operating in such a wide range of markets the business must handle such customer diversity on a daily basis. Satisfying so varied a customer base involves having a sound understanding of what product, sales and marketing attributes customers expect and need.

Companies vary in their ability to track customer histories and figures and even those which regularly update such records often fail to fully understand why customers make or do not make a particular purchase or enter into a relationship with a supplier.

In order to develop marketing programmes which strongly appeal to target customers, it is vital that companies fully appreciate the needs of their customer base. This means understanding the number, types and characteristics of customers in a particular market. In addition, businesses must have a clear view of the buying process which customers follow and understand the factors which influence them as they make a purchase. Related to this is the need to keep a close eye on emerging trends and identify current perceptions of different brands and patterns of supplier loyalty.

Keeping historical records of customer numbers and types has already been reviewed in Chapter 2 of this book, while section 9.3 will deal with reviewing customer perceptions of competing products and brands. The aims of this chapter are to review customer characteristics, consider the buying process and mechanics which customers go through when they buy, look at the factors which impact upon the buying decision and examine the product/service requirements (Key Customer Values or KCVs) of different customer types.

5.2 Understanding Customers

A clear understanding of customer needs and requirements is central to any marketing strategy or marketing planning programme. After all, the marketing concept relies on making the customer the focus of decision making. If companies are to capitalise on customer needs and take advantage of marketing opportunities, a detailed profile of those requirements is vital. For example, it is essential to understand the precise mix of product characteristics, service support, pricing and payment terms, delivery and promotion required by different types of customer. Any uncertainty in this area will probably result in less effective marketing programmes being developed.

As businesses review the needs of different customer types it is helpful for them to ask the following questions:

- What benefits are the customers seeking from the product or service? Which of these benefits are tangible and which are intangible? For example, a consumer who buys analgesic tablets may appreciate the tangible shape and texture of a product which make it easy to swallow, but the pain relief which the product brings is more intangible.
- Does the customer have any other needs which are related to the product or service in question? How do these affect the purchase decision? For example, computer software suppliers may be required to provide customers with appropriate training support.
- Is the purchase of any other product or service linked to that being reviewed? For example, a householder wishing to buy a number of materials and tools for some home maintenance, may expect to purchase all of the items in one store. This is likely to affect the type of outlet visited.
- What criteria does the customer consider when making the purchase decision? For example, how important are issues such as quality, delivery, service, price, product range, product innovation and the influence of promotional activity in the decision?
- What supplier criteria does the customer use when choosing what to buy?
- How does the customer go about searching for product or service information? For example, which media, publications, trade shows and exhibitions, word-of-mouth recommendations, etc, are used?
- What role does brand identity and awareness play? It may be easier

for a customer to seek brands with which they are familiar, rather than risk using an unknown supplier.

These questions provide answers which will assist in determining target markets and developing marketing programmes for them.

5.2.1 Key Customer Values

Some of the questions above relate specifically to customer needs, also called Key Customer Values (KCVs). KCVs are those factors expected and considered most important by customers. If these are not offered, the customer may not make a purchase, or may buy an alternative product which comes closer to matching the required KCVs. For example, garages and workshops which carry out car servicing and repairs are reliant on fast delivery and widespread availability of spare parts. Without these, the garages and workshops would not be able to operate efficiently.

An understanding of KCVs is essential if an organisation is to genuinely satisfy its targeted customers and endeavour to fend off its competitors. The 'voice of the customer' must be heard when determining product portfolios and new product development (NPD). Current NPD management practices such as quality functional deployment (QFD) depend on this knowledge of customer needs and expectations.

5.2.2 Customer Profiles

The design of effective marketing programmes is also contingent upon having a clear profile of the characteristics of different customer types. Many companies find that it is helpful to formally sketch a brief profile of different customer types at the same time as developing a list of KCVs. After all, the idea that certain customer characteristics are linked with specific needs and requirements is a core theme in effective marketing planning.

5.2.3 Buying Process and Influences

As well as having a sound appreciation of KCVs, selling organisations must properly understand how and why individual customers and organisations buy. After all, the mechanics of buying will inevitably impact upon the nature of customers' needs. Understanding the buying process and the mechanics (steps) involved helps companies to gear up their marketing efforts to more effectively influence the buying decision. For example, holiday companies know that the purchase of a family holiday is usually a protracted affair, and that a number of family members may be involved in the decision. It therefore makes sense to produce detailed brochures which can be used as the basis for extensive discussion. This is backed up with personal service through travel agents, who can answer any remaining queries. In short, by having a clear understanding of the buying process, providers are better able to develop a more suitable marketing mix (product, price, distribution, promotion and people) for the customers targeted.

5.3 The Behaviour and Buying Process of Customers

When discussing the behaviour and buying mechanics of customers, it is necessary to distinguish between individual and organisational buyers. Thus consumer buyer behaviour is said to be the decision processes and acts of individuals involved in buying and using products. Organisational (business to business) buyer behaviour is said to represent the purchase behaviour of other producers and resellers, government units and institutions.

5.3.1 Consumer Buying Decision Process

There have been many attempts to model or map out the way that consumers buy. Figure 5.1 illustrates a format which is typical of those which have been developed:

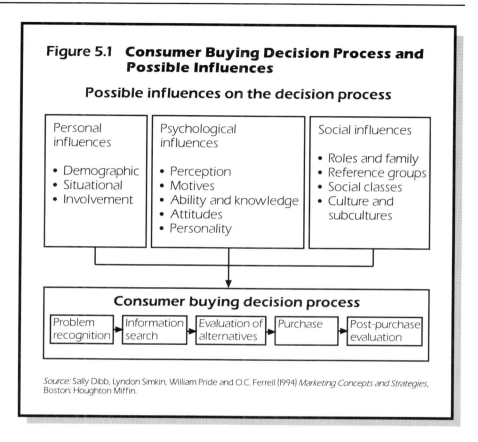

Figure 5.1 Consumer Buying Decision Process and Possible Influences

Possible influences on the decision process

Personal influences	Psychological influences	Social influences
• Demographic • Situational • Involvement	• Perception • Motives • Ability and knowledge • Attitudes • Personality	• Roles and family • Reference groups • Social classes • Culture and subcultures

Consumer buying decision process

Problem recognition → Information search → Evaluation of alternatives → Purchase → Post-purchase evaluation

Source: Sally Dibb, Lyndon Simkin, William Pride and O.C. Ferrell (1994) *Marketing Concepts and Strategies*, Boston: Houghton Miffin.

Briefly, the consumer buying decision process holds that consumers first recognise a problem or need for a product or service; they then search for information about relevant options (based on previous experiences, memory, KCVs, media and marketing influences); options are then evaluated against the KCVs/benchmarks set by each consumer; and the purchase is made (quickly for a routine purchase and with more care for a risky, expensive, or infrequently replaced item). The process does not end there, though, as many consumers go on to assess the performance and suitability of their purchase in a process known as post-purchase evaluation. The opinions which they form regarding product performance will influence the eventual replacement/renewal purchase.

There are a number of factors which *influence* the way in which people buy. By understanding some of these factors, businesses are in a better position to develop marketing programmes which cater for their customers. These influencing factors can be grouped in the following way:

- **Personal influences**: demographic issues (age/sex/occupation/income), situational factors (external conditions which exist when a purchase is made) and involvement (importance and attachment associated with the purchase).
- **Psychological influences**: consumers' different perceptions, motives and attitudes towards what and how they purchase. For example, many consumers' purchasing behaviour is now shaped by environmental concerns.
- **Social influences**: purchases made by consumers are influenced by a range of social factors. For example, individual tastes are influenced by social class and culture. Similarly, how consumers behave is affected by family roles and reference groups (friends and colleagues).
- **Media influences**: explicit marketing-led media activity such as advertising, sales promotion, publicity, sponsorship and direct mail obviously must influence purchase behaviour, but so do broadcast and print news, current affairs, drama and even light entertainment messages.

For example, a consumer purchasing a new pair of shoes will be influenced in a number of ways. Age, sex and income are all likely to impact upon the styles which are sought. The consumer may be swayed by the opinion of a friend or by a recent advertising campaign featuring a particular retail outlet.

It is clear then that there are benefits from understanding how and why consumers engage in buying. By mapping out the process in this step-by-step manner it is possible for businesses to obtain insights enabling them to refine the marketing efforts which are made at each stage of the buying decision.

5.3.2 The Organisational or Business to Business Buying Decision Process

Organisational markets can be classified into:

- **Industrial or producer markets**: these companies buy products for use in the manufacture of other products or to support that manufacture. For example, Nestlé buys a range of goods including glucose syrup/cocoa powder and sugar.

- **Reseller markets**: companies in this category buy goods for resale to customers. Generally they do not alter the physical nature of those goods, but they add value in terms of location/availability, warranty, service, parts support, relationships with customers. For example wholesalers or retailers, such as Marks and Spencer's or Aldi or JCB distributors/dealers. A sub-category includes those organisations which do not buy from a supplier, taking ownership, but which do sell on behalf of suppliers: agents, such as car franchisees. These companies generally deal in physical goods.
- **Institutional markets**: companies in this category include charities, libraries, hospitals, colleges.
- **Government markets**: this category includes both local and national government.
  Companies in these last two categories are generally involved with the handling of services.

This distinction into organisational type is important because it affects the characteristics of the buying process. For instance, government markets are known for their bureaucratic buying processes – often operating through a series of committees seeking tenders, taking many months.

Various attempts have been made to model the organisational buying decision process. Figure 5.2 is typical of the formats which have been developed.

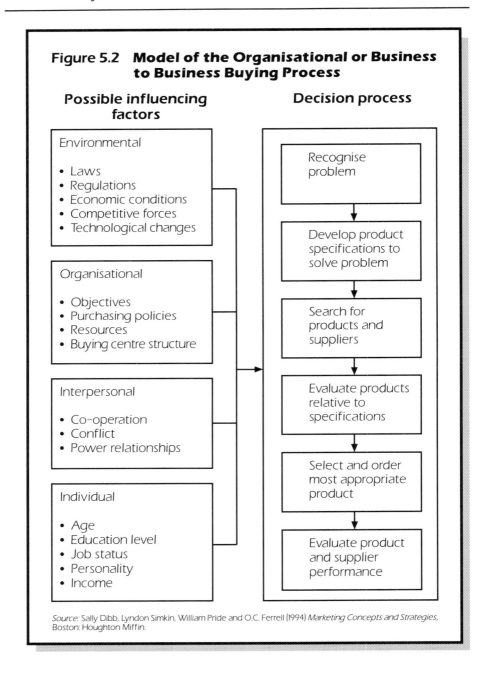

Figure 5.2 Model of the Organisational or Business to Business Buying Process

Possible influencing factors

Decision process

Environmental

- Laws
- Regulations
- Economic conditions
- Competitive forces
- Technological changes

Organisational

- Objectives
- Purchasing policies
- Resources
- Buying centre structure

Interpersonal

- Co-operation
- Conflict
- Power relationships

Individual

- Age
- Education level
- Job status
- Personality
- Income

Recognise problem

Develop product specifications to solve problem

Search for products and suppliers

Evaluate products relative to specifications

Select and order most appropriate product

Evaluate product and supplier performance

Source: Sally Dibb, Lyndon Simkin, William Pride and O.C. Ferrell (1994) *Marketing Concepts and Strategies*, Boston: Houghton Miffin.

The business to business buying decision process is similar to that for individual consumers, but is usually more formal. Once a need is recognised for a product or service, a specification is drawn up prior to a screening of potential suppliers. Those shortlisted suppliers are ranked and assessed in terms of costs, reliability/reputation, product know-how, service levels, so that a purchase decision can be made. Purchase is followed by post-purchase evaluation, when product/service and supplier performance are evaluated.

There is a range of factors which impact on and *influence* the nature of business to business buying and how that buying takes place. These include:

- **Environmental factors**: such as laws, regulations, economic conditions, social issues, competitive forces and technological change. For example, the impact of 1992 EC deregulation and more freedom to buy.
- **Organisational factors**: including company objectives (which may be short or long term), purchasing policies (such as 'Buy British'), resources, and the structure of the buying centre.
- **Interpersonal factors**: anyone involved in buying for an organisation will understand the power of relationships, conflict and co-operation which can impact on the decisions made.
- **Individual factors**: as in consumer buying, individual factors such as age, education level and job status will have an impact on the choices which are made.

For example, a manufacturing company seeking to construct a new factory must take into consideration a variety of factors. There will be a range of regulations and safety requirements which must be adhered to before and during the construction. The company may have a policy of seeking bids from more than one potential supplier, so that comparisons can be made. The previous experiences of members of the buying centre may also affect the suppliers which are shortlisted.

5.3.3 Comparing Business to Business and Consumer Buying

There are a number of obvious contrasts between consumer buying behaviour and the behaviour exhibited by businesses. These can be shown by highlighting the particular characteristics of organisational or business to business markets and approaches to buying.

Group activity

Generally more people are involved in organisational buying behaviour than in consumer buying behaviour. Those involved in buying in an organisational situation are collectively referred to as the *Buying Centre* and each individual will be responsible for particular buying roles. The number of people involved in buying will be organisation-specific, but usually relates to the type of purchase being made, the risk associated with it and time pressure. For example, a university department may require a particular clerical officer to order day-to-day stationery, but may involve a mix of more senior personnel when selecting new computer equipment.

High risk

Buying for organisations is usually more high risk than a consumer purchase. Risk in organisational purchases can come from high product value, the possible consequence of purchase, lack of knowledge about the product or service being bought, and uncertainty about the buying process or how to deal with suppliers.

Fewer and larger buyers

Fast Moving Consumer Goods (FMCG) companies tend to aim their products at mass markets but many companies in organisational markets are reliant on relatively few customers. This makes it more likely for long-term relationships to be developed, with companies seeking the benefits of reduced risk, trust, mutual adaptation and time saving. Such relationships are generally characterised by extensive use of personal selling (face to face contact).

Formal buying process

Organisational buyers are often restricted by certain company rules/procedures and have a fairly limited say in the purchase which is made. Some organisations are particularly bureaucratic. Generally, there is extensive use of formal quotes and tenders.

Nature of demand

Demand in organisational markets is derived from demand for products or services in consumer markets. This means it tends to fluctuate according to the level of demand for consumer goods. For example, the demand for glucose syrup is affected by the demand for confectionery.

Geographic concentration of buyers

There is a tendency for concentration of certain industries to occur in different areas. For example, in the UK information technology (IT) suppliers are now centred along the M4 motorway corridor.

5.4 Assessing Customers, KCVs and the Buying Process

At this stage in the analysis it is necessary to add to the historical and quantitative picture of customers developed in Chapter 2. For each type or group of customers a more qualitative profile is needed. Using a copy of Figure 5.3 for *each customer group or target market*, make a record of:

1. *The Buying Process Mechanics*: List the steps involved in the buying process (from the customer's viewpoint). What steps does the customer go through in order to make the purchase?

2. *The Core Influences*: Record any factors which have an influence on the buying decision being made. Which factors/issues influence *each* step in the process described (see 1)?

3. *Customer Profile*: Build up a picture of the typical characteristics of the customer type under review. Include any relevant personality, demographic, location, situational details.

4. *Key Customer Values*: Make a list of the KCVs required by each customer group (see Figure 2.1).

Figure 5.3 illustrates the buying process using the 35mm camera market as an example.

Figure 5.3 **Customers, KCVs, Buying Process Steps and Core Influences**

Example: 35mm camera market

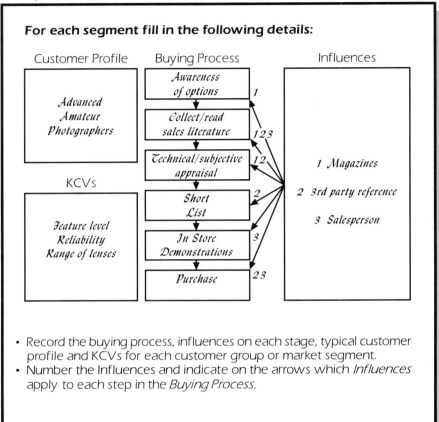

- Record the buying process, influences on each stage, typical customer profile and KCVs for each customer group or market segment.
- Number the Influences and indicate on the arrows which *Influences* apply to each step in the *Buying Process.*

5.5 Summary

This chapter helps to develop an understanding of customer needs and buying behaviour: essential for any successful marketing drive. This important area of marketing analysis is often overlooked, yet it provides a valuable insight into customers which goes further than simply considering product requirements. By examining the mechanics of buying it is possible to develop an entire marketing offering which is geared to satisfying customer requirements from the point at which unfulfilled need is recognised right up to the point of consumption. An appreciation of the core influences on buying should assist the business in determining which of these influences it is important to control. This additional understanding can be particularly important in markets where there is little variety in product needs or where competition is especially intense. In these circumstances, using buying behaviour characteristics to distinguish between different customer groups may offer an opportunity for developing a differential advantage over rivals.

6

Competition and Competitors' Strategies

6.1 Introduction

Any marketing planning programme must take full account of the prevailing competitive situation in which a company operates. There seems little doubt that marketing success is closely linked with becoming 'competitor-orientated'. Not surprisingly, successful marketing planning also relies on having a sound understanding of competitors' relative strengths and weaknesses, market shares and positions. By combining an appreciation of the competitive situation with key customer needs, organisations are better able to pinpoint attractive segments and position their product offerings. Closely monitoring change in the competitive arena helps organisations maintain control over their target market strategy and marketing plans. This chapter provides a framework for aggregating and summarising competitor information, assessing competitive positions and considering the needs satisfied and differential advantages offered by different market players.

6.2 Understanding the Competitive Arena

American management guru Michael Porter provides a useful approach for summarising the competitive arena which, he argues, consists of competing organisations jockeying for position in an environment determined by a number of outside forces. Figure 6.1 shows the different forces operating within the competitive arena.

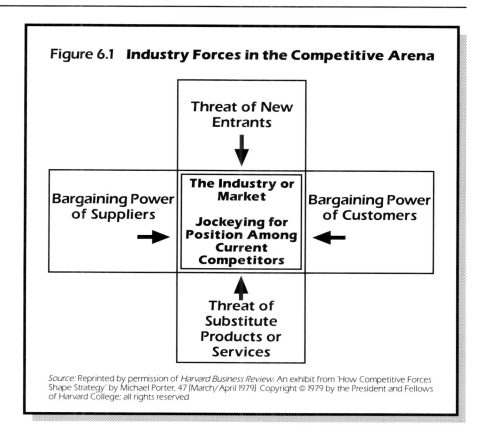

Figure 6.1 **Industry Forces in the Competitive Arena**

Bargaining power of suppliers

How much a particular supplier impacts on the situation depends on the availability of alternative suppliers and product substitutes. In monopoly situations the bargaining power of the supplier is particularly high and may be associated with high prices and inflexible, poor quality, product offerings. Many governments have attempted to break up traditional monopolies, such as the telecommunications industry, in order to reduce this form of bargaining power. At the other extreme, supplying companies in industries with many suppliers and much substitution frequently have quite low bargaining power.

Bargaining power of buyers

High buyer bargaining power usually occurs in industries where suppliers' power is low and where large volumes of standardised items can readily be sourced elsewhere. In many cases, for example the provision of certain raw materials to manufacturing industry, these items form only a part of the final product.

Threat of substitute products or services

A proliferation of substitute products within an industry can significantly limit the growth potential and long-term profits. This may result in competing companies having less control over price and facing overcapacity problems. For example, new technologies in the audio and hi-fi industry destroyed the market for vinyl records.

Threat of new entrants

New entrants in a market give increased capacity which can limit the market share or profits of existing competitors. The likely impact of new entrants is determined in part by any barriers to entry. Some typical barriers to entry include the presence of strongly branded competitors, economies of scale, control of distribution and high capital requirements. In markets where barriers are high, the number of new entrants will be limited. For example, Perkins is a leading UK based supplier of engines to construction and agricultural equipment manufacturers. Barriers to entry are high, so the reliance of many businesses on Perkins is great.

In order to compete effectively within this competitive arena, Porter suggests there are three bases on which to compete. An organisation which *fails* to master any one of these is *un*likely to have the strengths with which to fend off competitors:

- **Cost leadership**: Low cost base through scale economies – Toyota's approach.
- **Differentiation**: Unique product or marketing offer: innovative product, service, branding, distribution or pricing – Caterpillar in construction equipment aims to be a 'one stop shop' through its extensive product range and distribution coverage.
- **Focus**: Often smaller companies unable to opt for *Cost* or *Differentiation* specialise on tightly defined markets – Cray Computers builds only super computers targeted at just a few customers.

6.3 Warfare Strategies

The analysis of competition and the development of competitive strategies have also been linked to military principles. Under this scenario, competing companies represent the *enemy* which must be defeated. In any market or market segment, there are said to be four different types of competitive position which companies can occupy. Which position a company occupies, and how this fits in with what the competition is doing, will impact on the strategy which that company should follow.

6.3.1 Competitive Positions

There are five possible positions for an organisation.

Market leader
This is the highest market share company which retains its position by trying to expand the total market, perhaps by finding new uses for a product, or increasing market share (market penetration), for example through an aggressive advertising campaign. It is necessary for companies like Coca-Cola and McDonald's, which occupy leading positions, to achieve a balance between aggressively seeking new market share while protecting their existing position.

Market challenger
This position is occupied by one or more non-market leaders which *aggressively* attack for additional market share. In the soft drinks market Pepsi occupies this position.

Fast movers
These are not the major players in a market, but they are growing and attempting to win a share. They will not in the short term challenge for leadership, but they are gaining at the expense of rivals. The airline Virgin is such an example.

Market follower
These are low share competitors without the resources/market position/R&D/commitment to challenge or seriously contend for market leadership. Instead they are happy to settle for a smaller share of the market and may concentrate efforts on a constrained area of the market.

Market nicher
Companies which specialise in terms of market/product/customers by finding a safe, profitable market segment. As markets mature, increasing competitiveness forces larger rivals to target such segments,

making life difficult for the nicher. Retailer Body Shop initially captured a hold in the cosmetics market by identifying a niche for environmentally friendly and cruelty-free policies. Companies which commit all their resources to one niche market can find themselves particularly susceptible in such circumstances.

An understanding of competitive positions is important because different marketing strategies are appropriate depending upon the competitive position. Nichers specialise and are narrowly focused. Market leaders have to fend off competitors' attacks while continuing plans to develop and grow their markets. Challengers are aggressive but must only attack the leader's and other challengers' weak points: head-on moves will most likely be costly. Followers are the 'me-toos' in the market place: they copy other players' successes. The various marketing strategies may be based either on attacking or defensive moves.

6.3.2 Principles of Defensive Warfare Strategies

The skill to adopt a defensive position is important if companies are to protect their existing market share. However, defence should not be regarded solely as a negative activity. Strong defence involves striking a balance between waiting to be attacked and pre-empting aggressive competitive moves. In general, only the market leader should consider adopting a defensive role, but even for this player, it is essential to combine defensive and offensive strategies. History is littered with the remains of companies which fell into a false sense of security about their market position and left themselves open to attack from aggressive market challengers. Such companies should remember that adopting a defensive position does not necessarily mean remaining static; they should be ready to move and respond to aggressive marketing effort from competitors. Defence still presents several options:

- Build walls around strong positions. This requires companies to fully understand their true strengths (for example, brand name), and to be proactive in their attempts to retain those strengths. For example, car company Rover has done much to build on traditions of the Rover brand, by changing its policy to incorporate it into all of its product range.
- Protect weak areas. Attention on weak areas can sometimes be diverted by marketing tactics which focus on other aspects of the product/marketing offering. For example, a supplier of highly

priced electronic components may seek to emphasis product quality in its marketing.

- Be mobile and ready to move. Companies should be quick to exploit new markets, products and opportunities. Virgin Atlantic airlines has been proactive in seeking new route opportunities.
- Withdrawal from market/product if absolutely necessary. It can be sensible to consolidate in areas which are strong, thus focusing resources. Such action should not leave weak areas which might allow competitors access to key markets.

6.3.3 Principles of Offensive Warfare Strategies

The principles of offensive warfare are particularly relevant to companies in a non-market leading position, which are challenging aggressively for additional market share. It is often regarded as lower risk to attack market followers and market nichers rather than the market leading organisation, but this depends on the strength of the leader's position. Attacking companies must beware of the dangers of antagonising powerful, resource-rich market leaders. If the leader is to be attacked, the challenging organisation must find a weakness in the leader's strength and attack at that point. Launching the attack on a narrow front tends to increase the chances of success. The challenger should be sure that it has the resources to sustain the attack for as long as necessary.

- Head to head. This full frontal method of attack is in many ways the most difficult to sustain and only the most powerful challengers should attempt it. The attack involves attempting to match the market leader blow by blow on some aspect of the marketing programme (for example, supermarkets Sainsbury and Tesco periodically engage in price wars with each other). Challengers which attempt this approach often fail!
- Attack weak points. This approach to attack requires the challenger to identify and match its key areas of strength and weakness against the market leader. Efforts can then be pitched against points of particular weakness. Burger King targeted the standardised McDonald's offerings with a 'Have it your way' campaign, where the consumer was encouraged to ask for their burger any way they wanted it.
- Adopt a multi-pronged strategy. It can be appropriate to overwhelm competitor, with several points of attack (for example, combining

a promotional programme with new product innovation) and thus diluting competitors' ability to respond.

■ Guerrilla attack. This type of challenging is not large scale and prolonged. The intention is to annoy competitors with unpredictable and periodic attacks.

6.3.4 Strategies for Market Followers and Nichers

Although there are opportunities for *followers* in markets, as Amstrad showed in the personal computer market, companies occupying these positions are often vulnerable to attack from their larger competitors. In order to minimise the risks of such attack market followers should use market segmentation carefully, concentrating only on areas where the company can cope. It is also helpful to specialise rather than diversify so that resources are not spread too thinly. This means the emphasis is on profitability rather than sales growth. Using R&D as efficiently as possible can also help ensure that resources are used in the most appropriate manner.

In many markets, *nichers* are the most vulnerable competitors. They must avoid competition with other organisations in order to ensure their success, particularly as markets become more mature. This can be achieved by seeking safe market segments, typically in areas where big companies do not believe it is worth competing. Such niches may be secured by specialising on a particular market, customer or marketing mix. However, nichers must avoid becoming over committed to one small area of the market. This can be achieved by being strong in more than one niche. If there is an aggressive attack on one niche segment, this means that there may be opportunities to switch resources to another.

6.4 Monitoring Competitors' Strategies

Irrespective of the market in which a business operates, some understanding of competitors' strategies is of fundamental importance. It should not be too difficult to review competitors' past actions, product launches, price campaigns, distribution policies, promotional campaigns, press releases; their reaction to the business's own product launches or modifications to sales and marketing programmes. Many companies are surprisingly predictable and building a profile of their activities allows the business to forecast how their competitors might respond in future. For example, a European telecommunications equipment manufacturer was able to predict the response of several key competitors to one of its marketing programmes. One potential difficulty in this area is that although managers may know a lot about their competitors – from chance discussions, press comment, industry gossip, dealer feedback, the sales force – these insights may not be shared with colleagues until it is too late. With an 'ear to the ground', much marketing intelligence can be gathered about competitors at low cost. The following areas should receive attention:

- product and pricing activities;
- dealer and customer service moves;
- major account purchases or account moves;
- likely reaction to the business's moves; and
- reactions to changes in the trading environment.

6.5 Recording Competitive Positions and Strengths

As explained in Chapter 5 (5.2), it is important to understand the product, sales and marketing attributes customers expect and need. In terms of a competitor analysis, it is also important to know which Key Customer Values (KCVs) each competitor is believed to offer or deliver, and whether in so doing any competitor gains a differential or competitive advantage in the marketplace over its rivals. A differential advantage – or competitive edge – is something a company or its product has, which is desired by the target market, and is not currently readily matched by rival companies or products. The concept builds from the 'unique selling proposition' or USP so popular with sales managers in the 1970s. By understanding the advantages which competitors offer, a business will be better placed to develop and fine-tune its own marketing effort. For example, Adams Childrenswear undertook a review of customer perceptions of key retailers in its market. As a result the company repositioned itself to offer good quality, fashionable and reasonably priced clothing.

Figure 6.2, which is illustrated using the 35mm camera market provides a summary grid of competitive information per segment. It:

1. aggregates information regarding the competitors and positions occupied within each target market or segment;

2. considers the KCVs met or offered by *competitors*; and

3. examines whether the KCVs delivered in each market constitute a differential/competitive advantage.

Figure 6.2 Competitive Positions and Differential Advantage

Example: 35mm camera market

Competitive Position	Segment:	Segment:	Segment:
Market Leader:	*NIKON*	-	-
• Market Share Change	+	-	-
• KCVs Offered	*RELIABILITY*	-	-
		-	-
• DA (if any)	*LENS RANGE*	-	-
Challenger 1:	*CANON*	-	-
• Market Share Change	+ +	-	-
• KCVs Offered	*PERFORMANCE*	-	-
		-	-
• DA (if any)	*SPECIFICATION*	-	-
Challenger 2:	*MINOLTA*	-	-
• Market Share Change	+	-	-
• KCVs Offered	*PERFORMANCE*	-	-
		-	-
• DA (if any)	*TECHNOLOGY*	-	-
Challenger 3:	-	-	-
• Market Share Change	-	-	-
• KCVs Offered	-	-	-
	-	-	-
• DA (if any)	-	-	-
Fast Mover:	-	-	-
• Market Share Change	-	-	-
• KCVs Offered	-	-	-
	-	-	-
• DA (if any)	-	-	-
Follower:	*PENTAX*	-	-
• Market Share Change		-	-
• KCVs Offered		-	-
		-	-
• DA (if any)		-	-
Nicher:	*LEICA*	-	-
• Market Share change		-	-
• KCVs Offered	*PERFORMANCE*	-	-
		-	-
• DA (if any)	*QUALITY*	-	-

· Record the competitive positions for each segment
· The KCVs on this chart are those KCVs that each competitor is able to match
· Most companies do not have a DA (differential advantage), so this slot may be left blank for many companies
· There is *no* need to list actual %s for market share changes, current year versus last year. Key to market share entries: ++ large market share increase; + small market share increase; − small market share decline; −− large market share decline

6.6 **Summary**

This chapter aims to build an overview of the competitive arena in which organisations operate. The impact of a business's marketing strategy is shaped by the actions of various competitive players and the way in which each strives to match key customer values. It is important to understand how competitors will react to the business's target market strategy and associated marketing plan programmes.

No business can operate in isolation of its competitors' moves and it is vital to anticipate their reactions. Many companies behave in a surprisingly 'predictable' manner. Examining their recent past and marketing initiatives should give a reasonable clue to their forth-coming moves and their reaction to the business's planned marketing programmes. It should be possible to 'second guess' how rivals will behave. It is also important to realise which competitors are effective or ineffective at matching target customers' needs, as this will reveal rivals' strengths and weaknesses in terms of satisfying customers, possibly presenting the business with opportunities or some threats.

7

The Strength of the Portfolio: Future Directions

7.1 Introduction

Section II has so far examined the core background analyses which lead to a sound understanding of a market. The final two background marketing analyses concern the business's mix of products. It is essential to have products (or services) which assist the business in maximising its opportunities and which conform with key customer needs. No company has a portfolio of totally successful products: there will be some which are on the decline, with others still to realise their potential, while a few will be the company's cash cows. It is important for the business to realise which products are its bread and butter, which need to be nurtured and which are an unhealthy drain on resources. Various approaches have been developed to help companies manage their portfolios of products.

This chapter presents the directional policy matrix (DPM), a widely adopted tool for managing the product portfolio. The chapter also reviews the product life cycle concept which holds that all products have a life, passing from birth, into growth, to maturity and ultimately into decline. An understanding of this issue is vital if a business is to fully appreciate the current standing and future potential of the markets in which it operates.

7.2 The Balanced Portfolio

7.2.1 The Directional Policy Matrix Approach to Assessing Business Position and Market Attractiveness

The aim of the *Market Attractiveness/Business Position Matrix* (or the DPM) is to assess the relative attractiveness of investing in particular businesses, so as to determine appropriate strategic planning goals and appropriate funding/manpower. 'Business' can be taken to mean an SBU (strategic business unit), a product group, an individual product or segment. For the purpose of this chapter, the term SBU will be used, although individual businesses must decide upon the most appropriate level of analysis for them. For example, typically companies set up SBUs on the basis of core product groups or territories, but for the purposes of this exercise it may be more appropriate to use market segments (perhaps in conjunction with territories, for organisations with international markets).

A company reviews the performance of each of its SBUs in the context of the company's overall portfolio. The relative 'health'/ potential of each SBU enables the company to decide which SBUs to '*build*' (develop further/increase market share), '*maintain*' (resource to keep the status quo/current market share), '*harvest*' (sell-off/pull out of after squeezing the last potential sales), or '*divest*'/sell (drop more or less immediately).

Most managers intuitively know which products are yesterday's 'has-beens' or tomorrow's 'breadwinners'. Managerial impressions, though, are rarely sufficient or robust enough as a basis for such fundamental decision making. Hence, the development of such analytical techniques by the major consultancies (McKinsey, Boston Consultancy Group) and blue chip companies, such as General Electric. For example, an education consultancy providing executive management courses became aware of the poor financial contribution and declining popularity of one of its short programmes, but was uncertain how to proceed. Using portfolio management techniques enhanced the business's understanding of the shape of its overall portfolio and clarified decision making about the future of the programme.

7.2.2 Assessing Market Attractiveness and Business Position

1. For each SBU decide which **factors** are the **most appropriate** for assessing the *market attractiveness*. This should be assessed relative to the market as a whole.

2. Separately, repeat for the *business position* (sometimes called the competitive position or relative business strength). This is assessed relative to the leading/strongest competitor or relative market share.

These decisions are usually based on the informed judgement of management taking into consideration any relevant research information. Generally, it is best not to exceed five or six factors. For example, when assessing market attractiveness, one company manufacturing agricultural equipment uses four: industry sales, growth rate, market share, and profitability. A full list of the kinds of variables which can be used in this analysis is shown in Figure 7.1.

Figure 7.1 Variables for Assessing Market Attractiveness and Business Position

Attractiveness of your market	Status/position of your business
Market factors	
Size (money, units or both)	Your share (in equivalent terms)
Size of key segments	Your share of key segments
Growth rate per year:	Your annual growth rate:
total	total
segments	segments
Diversity of market	Diversity of your participation
	Brand awareness image
Sensitivity to price, service features	Your influence on the market
and external factors	
Cyclicality	Lags or leads in your sales
Seasonality	
Bargaining power of upstream suppliers	Bargaining power of your suppliers
Bargaining power of downstream	Bargaining power of your customers
suppliers	
Competition	Where you fit, how you compare in
Types of competitors	terms of products, marketing capability,
Degree of concentration	service, production strength, financial
Changes in type and mix	strength, management
Entries and exits	Segments you have entered or left
Changes in share	Your relative share change
Substitution by new technology	Your vulnerability to new technology
Degrees and types of integration	Your own level of integration
Financial and economic factors	Your margins
Contribution margins	Your scale and experience
Leveraging factors, such as economies of	
scale and experience	Barriers to your entry or exit (both
Barriers to entry or exit (both financial and	financial and non-financial)
non-financial)	Your capacity utilisation
Capacity utilisation	
Technological factors	Your ability to cope with change
Maturity and volatility	Depths of your skills
Complexity	Types of your technological skills
Differentiation	Your patent protection
Patents and copyrights	Your manufacturing technology
Manufacturing process technology required	
Socio-political factors in your	Your company's responsiveness and
environment	flexibility
Social attitudes and trends	Your company's ability to cope
Laws and government agency regulations	
Influence with pressure groups and	Your company's aggressiveness
government representatives	Your company's relationships
Human factors, such as unionisation and	
community acceptance	

Source: M.H.B. McDonald (1989) *Marketing Plans: How to Prepare Them, How to Use Them*, Oxford: Butterworth-Heinemann, 102-3

3. Once the two lists of factors have been derived for the market attractiveness and business position, decide how important each of the factors is and allocate an appropriate **weighting**. The total weighting should add up to 100 for each list. For example, when considering market attractiveness, market size may be seen to be a particularly important factor and be allocated a weighting of 50. Profitability and rate of market growth, which are seen as less important, might receive weightings of 30 and 20 respectively.

4. Next, give a **score** to each factor which reflects how the particular SBU under consideration shapes up relative to other SBUs. One simple and effective way to do this is to make 0.0 = low/poor, 0.5 = medium/average, and 1.0 = high/good.

5. Multiply the weighting by the score to give a **ranking** for each factor. The **sum** of the rankings for each SBU analysed should then be calculated and recorded.

6. Repeat the process for other SBUs, until all have been evaluated.

7. Enter each SBU position on the matrix using a circle. The diameter of the circle usually reflects the sales volume of the SBU. Alternatively the circle's diameter can refer to the market size. Whichever is chosen, ensure consistency throughout the analysis. If market size is used an area of the circle can be shaded to show the market share of the SBU (as in Figure 7.2). Remember that the analysis can be undertaken at the level of segment, territory, product group or product. SBU is only used here to illustrate the mechanics of the process.

7.2.3 Worked Example

The following worked example helps to demonstrate the operation of the DPM approach.

Market Attractiveness

Factor	Score	Weighting	Ranking (Scale 1–100)
Market size	0.5	25	12.5
Volume growth (units)	0.0	10	0.0
Level of competition	1.0	40	40.0
Market diversity	1.0	25	25.0
		100	77.5

Business Strength/Competitive Position

Factor	Score	Weighting	Ranking (Scale 1–100)
Product technology			
– quality	1.0	30	30.0
– new technology	0.5	10	5.0
Marketing			
– share of key segments	0.0	20	0.0
– service back-up	1.0	15	15.0
Manufacturing			
– efficiency	0.0	10	0.0
– technology	0.5	15	7.5
		100	57.5

The total market attractiveness and business position ratings (77.5 and 57.5 respectively) make up the co-ordinates on the DPM chart.

7.2.4 Interpreting the DPM

Interpreting the DPM requires that the user follows a series of simple procedures. Figure 7.2 shows an example of a completed matrix and Figure 7.3 the outline strategies to follow.

In general those SBUs or products appearing in the top left of the chart can be deemed as the 'star' products or businesses. Those SBUs or products which appear in the bottom left of the chart, typically will be the 'cash cows' for the company (those products on which the company depends for the bulk of its income/cash generation).

SBUs/segments/products floating around in the centre and top right of the chart tend to be those for which the future is uncertain (in other words over which there is a question mark). For these SBUs/segments/products a decision must be made on whether to cut losses and cease production or to put full marketing/distributor resources behind a major push.

SBUs/segments/products which are located in the bottom right of the chart are the real 'dogs' in the portfolio, with very little potential and probably already making losses. These 'dog' products should be dropped immediately or in the very near future.

7.2.5 Levels of Analysis

As has already been indicated, companies tend to undertake this type of portfolio analysis at a number of different levels. Indeed, some businesses see the benefits of applying the approach in a variety of ways. For example, businesses may choose to begin by reviewing the product group level, then move on to consider all product groups, for the company as a whole, segment by segment. The analysis could also be undertaken company-wide for all individual products, for certain product groups/SBUs, for individual products, for specific market segments, separate countries, certain dealer types, or for any permutation.

When deciding upon a level of analysis, businesses must remember that the concept is intended to look at a company's portfolio and its value.

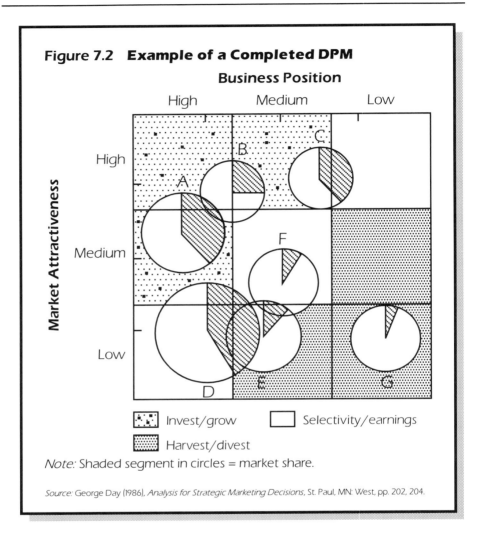

Figure 7.2 Example of a Completed DPM

Note: Shaded segment in circles = market share.

Source: George Day (1986), *Analysis for Strategic Marketing Decisions*, St. Paul, MN: West, pp. 202, 204.

Figure 7.3 Strategy Implications from DPM Positions

Market Attractiveness	Strong	Medium	Weak
High	**Protect Position** • invest to grow at maximum digestible rate • concentrate effort on maintaining strength	**Invest to Build** • challenge for leadership • build selectively on strengths • reinforce vulnerable areas	**Build Selectively** • specialise around limited strengths • seek ways to overcome weaknesses • withdraw if indications of sustainable growth are lacking
Medium	**Build Selectively** • invest heavily in most attractive segments • build up ability to counter competition • emphasise profitability by raising productivity	**Selectivity/Manage for Earnings** • protect existing programme • concentrate investments in segments where profitability is good and risk is relatively low	**Limited Expansion or Harvest** • look for ways to expand without high risk; otherwise, minimise investment and rationalise operations
Low	**Protect and Refocus** • manage for current earnings • concentrate on attractive segments • defend strengths	**Manage for Earnings** • protect position in most profitable segments • upgrade product line • minimise investment	**Divest** • sell at time that will maximise cash value • cut fixed costs and avoid investment meanwhile

Business Position

Source: George Day (1986), *Analysis for Strategic Marketing Decisions*, St. Paul, MN: West, pp. 202, 204.

7.2.6 Recording the Portfolio Analysis

The factors which make a market attractive need to be determined, scored, weighted and ranked, as in the example above, similarly the factors which the business feels affect the business position. Figure 7.4 presents a grid for pulling this information together.

Figure 7.4 **Information Required for the DPM Analysis**

Market Attractiveness			
Factors	**Score**	**Weighting**	**Ranking**

Business/Competitive Position			
Factors	**Score**	**Weighting**	**Ranking**

- Select the factors felt to be most important. Complete the columns
- This information now needs to be plotted on a graph, 7.5, as in Figure 7.2

What are the Implications from this Analysis?

Figure 7.5 The DPM

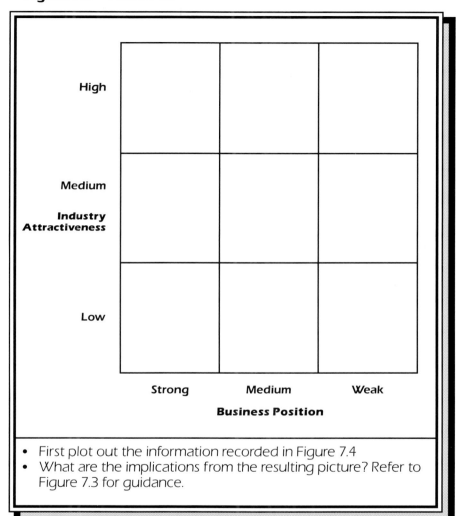

- First plot out the information recorded in Figure 7.4
- What are the implications from the resulting picture? Refer to Figure 7.3 for guidance.

7.3 The Product Life Cycle (PLC)

Marketing theory suggests that most products or services have a 'life cycle', similar to people. According to this theory, products are born (created) and introduced into the market. There is a growth period as consumer interest and sales increase. After a period of growth, products reach steady state, often referred to as maturity. Eventually, the products will lose their appeal and sales decline, effectively signalling the end of maturity and the death of the product. This product life cycle (PLC) can be represented by a sales growth curve and industry profit graph as shown in Figure 7.6.

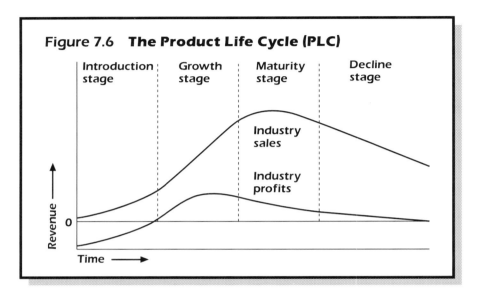

Figure 7.6 **The Product Life Cycle (PLC)**

The product life cycle can be applied at a number of different levels. Taking cars as an example of a product category, hatchbacks as a product variant and the Mondeo as a particular model, each has its own life cycle, although the concept is, perhaps, most widely applied at the model (or brand) level. Marketers who have a sound understanding of typical life-cycle patterns are more likely to maintain profitable products while dropping unprofitable ones. This is increasingly important due to generally shorter life cycles in many markets, led by fast moving customer requirements and competitive activity, making it difficult for some companies to recover NPD and R&D costs during the model's life cycle. The product life cycle also has implications for the business's cash flow which typically peaks in the maturity stage and will impact on the scope of the marketing activity undertaken.

7.3.1 The Introduction Stage

Estimates of the success rate for new products vary. Some figures suggest that between 33 per cent and 90 per cent of all new products fail. During the introduction stage it is vital that buyers are made aware of the product and their direct interest kindled. Development and marketing costs will be high. Prices also are usually set at a high level, but even so spiralling costs often result in negative profits.

The marketer can adopt a number of introduction strategies. Under the rapid skimming approach, the product is introduced with high price and high sales and advertising support, with the intention of achieving the greatest possible revenue per unit sold. For example, exclusive fashion houses may adopt this approach for very fashionable clothing which has only a short life cycle. With slow skimming, the sale price is high, but promotional support is lower. Revenue is required quickly, but costs must be kept down. A useful approach when the market size is expected to be small, the potential buyers are eager and competition is minimal.

For rapid penetration, there is high spending on promotion, but the price is relatively low: the aim is to achieve a fast take-off and large market share. This is an appropriate way forward if the market is large, unaware of the product, if competition is likely and if buyers are price sensitive. Airlines often use this approach when offering services on new routes. For slow penetration, there is low price with low promotional support to gain rapid market acceptance at low cost to the company.

7.3.2 The Growth Stage

During this stage there is a rapid increase in sales. Profits can be seen to peak – as manufacturing and marketing costs are spread across more sales – and then decline as more competitors enter the booming market to 'ride on the back' of those companies which have created the market. Price cutting can occur as competition increases.

The strategy in the growth stage aims to maintain growth as long as possible through improving product quality, adding new features, moving into additional market segments, using new distribution channels, altering promotion or revising prices. These approaches can improve a company's competitive position, but all have cost implications. The business strives, though, for longer term gains.

7.3.3 The Maturity Stage

Throughout the maturity stage, competition intensifies. Competitors are forced to offer improved products with shrewder marketing programmes. Sales peak, then level off – the plateau in the PLC. Companies engage in increased promotional activity to stave off impending decline. Almost inevitably, profits decline as competition intensifies, more products are added to ranges and promotional costs rise. For example, the washing powder market, dominated by Lever Brothers and Proctor & Gamble has become increasingly fragmented, with numerous new product variants and brands introduced, backed up with expensive promotional campaigns.

The maturity stage lasts longer than the others so is often sub-divided into growth maturity, stable maturity and decaying maturity. The slow down in sales leads to over capacity and declining profits. Competition intensifies with price cutting and heavy advertising. Some weaker competitors drop out of the market. For the more entrenched companies, the task is to attain a distinct differential or competitive advantage. Maximum cash flow is often in this stage.

Surviving companies opt for one or a mixture of three approaches:

a) Market modification involves converting non-users, entering new segments or winning market share from competitors. Sometimes volumes can be increased by finding new uses for the product or by encouraging more frequent purchase.

b) Product modification, with new features or quality improvements to attract more usage or new users.

c) Marketing mix modification to stimulate sales by manipulating pricing, promotion, service or distribution.

7.3.4 The Decline Stage

Eventually sales will decline rapidly. This can be because of changing customer tastes, competing substitute products, social concerns, legislation, media coverage or corporate policies. Companies face severe competition coupled with declining revenues. Product port-folios will require rationalisation, and at some point, the decision may be made to divest from the market entirely.

Strategies are relatively few: weak products must be identified and withdrawn from the market. Market share, sales, profits and contri-butions will make this decision reasonably obvious, if far from palatable. When the product is dropped, the company must decide whether to sell it on to a different supplier, transfer it over or kill it off completely. Decisions must also be made as to whether the product should be phased out quickly or slowly. For example, changing technology has led to a shift in purchasing patterns in the recorded music industry: vinyl records, once the mainstay of the industry, are now only available in a limited number of outlets, with compact discs and tapes occupying the vast majority of shelf space.

7.3.5 The PLC in Marketing Planning

The PLC is a useful concept in planning, as a control mechanism for marketing activities, and in sales forecasting. In the context of marketing planning, the PLC helps to identify the main challenges facing each product. Where a product is sold to more than one customer group or in more than one territory, the product life cycle position of that product may vary. For example, many business schools around the world offer MBA (master of business administration) qualifications, yet in America, the market is much more mature (possibly even declining) than in Europe or Scandinavia. Understanding these variations in PLC positions, product by product and market by market, is vital if businesses are to develop appropriate marketing strategies (Section III) and marketing programmes for implementation (Section IV): Figure 7.7.

Figure 7.7   **The Stages of the PLC**

Segment and Product	PLC Stage	Implications

- For each product in each segment indicate the stage in the PLC reached – in column 2
- In column 3, suggest the more obvious strategic implications for each product

7.4 Summary

The directional policy matrix (DPM) can be used to assess the health of the business in terms of the balance of the product portfolio. By reviewing the performance of each product or product group, decisions can be made about areas in which to invest. With the knowledge of customers' needs and competitors' ability to match these, the product portfolio can be managed within the marketing planning initiative to good effect. Cash draining areas can be identified so that, if necessary, a disinvestment strategy also can be followed. The DPM is useful for examining the health of the current portfolio of products as well as for longer term planning in selecting attractive markets of the future.

The product life cycle (PLC) concept is similarly useful for contributing to the diagnosis of problem areas and guiding marketing strategy and the development of marketing programmes on a product by product and market by market basis.

Section II Checklist

By the end of this *Core Analyses* section of *The Marketing Planning Workbook* you should have:
- Reviewed the nature and value of existing markets
- Examined the market trends and issues of the marketing environment
- Conducted a SWOT analysis
- Analysed customer needs, expectations and buying processes
- Studied the competitive situation and competitors' strategies
- Assessed the strength and balance of the business's product portfolio
- Reviewed the product life cycle positions of the product portfolio

These are the essential background marketing analyses without which it is difficult to make sound strategic decisions and risky to produce marketing mix recommendations.

The Marketing Planning Workbook

Section I
Perspective

Section II
Core Analyses

Section III
Analyses into Strategy

Section IV
Programmes for Implementation

Section V
The Marketing Plan Document

Section III

Analyses into Strategy – Marketing Strategy Summary

Once complete, the core marketing analyses provide an up-to-date view of the marketplace and the business's position within it. On the basis of such marketing intelligence a business must determine which are its core target markets and how it expects to be perceived within these markets in relation to its rivals. The identification of target markets and positioning of the business's offerings within them is the next stage of the marketing planning process. Success depends on the business's ability to specify a clear marketing strategy to facilitate this target market selection and positioning. This marketing strategy must maximise the business's strengths and differential advantages whenever possible and should relate to the organisation's mission statement. Section III discusses the strategic aspects of marketing planning.

■ Mission statement
■ Target markets/segments
■ Targeting
■ Brand positioning
■ Strategy statement
■ Marketing objectives
■ Gaps hindering implementation

8

Marketing Strategy

8.1 Introduction

There are four key components to the marketing strategy section of marketing planning: the determination of market segments, the choice of which market segments the business wishes to target with bespoke products and marketing programmes, the basis on which to compete in each target market, and finally, the desired brand positioning in the minds of the targeted customers versus competitors. These strategic decisions need to be taken within the context of the business's mission statement.

It is essential that the recommended marketing strategy within the marketing plan reflects fully the information and market situation presented by the marketing analyses outlined in Section II of this workbook. It is unrealistic to believe that pre-existing marketing strategy choices will suffice in the light of the updated marketing intelligence. This chapter begins by considering the mission statement of the business and then gives some marketing strategy background before explaining the first two components: market segmentation and the selection of target markets.

8.2 Mission or Purpose Statement

Most businesses have a stated mission statement summing up their sense of purpose. If there is not one already defined, now is a good opportunity to define it given the knowledge of the business's markets and position versus rivals determined from the core marketing analyses. Where a mission statement does exist, it is likely to have been developed by senior management not as aware of core trends and issues identified by the analysis of the marketplace detailed in Section II of this book. For these reasons it may now be necessary to modify and update the material. Whatever the existing situation, the stated sense of purpose in the organisation's mission statement must be incorporated in the marketing function's thinking as strategies are finalised within marketing planning. The recommended strategies, and ultimately the associated programmes for implementation, must relate to the business's stated purpose.

Mission statements tend to fall into one of several categories. First, there are the very broad statements often found in annual reports:

> *This company strives for perfection in its product development, customer service and commitment to the natural environment.*

> *The company will become the leading supplier of detergents in Europe through acquisition and prudent use of resources.*

Such 'motherhood' statements may keep the media and shareholders happy, but otherwise are relatively meaningless in terms of marketing actions. More appropriate is the second type, a meaningful statement unique to the organisation which impacts on the behaviour of all executives and personnel, affecting sales and marketing decisions.

Third, there is a functional statement derived by the marketing function and appropriate to a business unit or to one product group. For example, JCB dominates the European market for construction equipment, but in large crawler excavators it is a relatively minor player. The mission for this product group is to take leadership in the UK market, make significant, specified inroads in certain other territories, while establishing a presence, no matter how small, in other stated territories in Europe. A very different situation from that faced by the company's other product groups, many of which are dominant in Europe.

As a general rule the mission statement should include, in less than a page:

- Stated role: profit (contribution), service, opportunities sought; immediate priorities and medium term goals.
- Business definition: in terms of customer needs, benefits provided – not only the products produced.
- Company strengths, advantages, marketing assets: qualities which create the foundation for the organisation's fortunes and ability to service markets.

Using Figure 8.1, state the business's mission statement as it impacts on the marketing function.

Figure 8.1 *Mission Statement Summary*

Summary of the Business's Mission or Purpose
Corporate Mission Statement for the Business:
Mission Statement Relating to the Marketing Function:
• Use Figure 8.1 to (a) summarise the overall stated corporate mission – or sense of purpose – for the business, and (b) put this into a marketing context in terms of required marketing objectives

8.3 Target Markets

Marketing plans ultimately lead to marketing programmes based on the marketing mix. If the plan is to be successful in this respect, it must be based on a clear target market strategy and emphasise any advantages over competitors.

Having analysed the market, the business must therefore turn its improved understanding of the market's activities and requirements into a clear strategy statement. This, essentially, involves identifying the markets to target, any differential advantages for the business's products, and the required product or service positionings.

8.4 Market Segmentation

8.4.1 Why Segment?

A proper understanding of the varying needs and requirements of different customers is fundamental to the principles of marketing. Although companies may recognise the breadth of such needs it is unrealistic to customise products to suit each individual, unless concentrating on a niche market. Moving away from mass marketing or, at the other extreme, bespoke customised services, towards a market segmentation approach where the focus is on a particular group (or groups) of customers, is an increasingly popular way of dealing with this diversity of needs. Additionally, by adopting a different segmentation approach than rivals, a business can gain an edge over competitors in servicing targeted customers' needs.

Many companies believe that marketing success is linked to how effectively their customer base is segmented. This is because market segmentation allows companies to go some of the way towards satisfying diverse customer needs while maintaining certain scale economies. The process begins by grouping together customers with similar requirements and buying characteristics. Next, the organisation can select the group(s) on which to target its sales, marketing and brands. A marketing programme can then be designed to cater for the specific requirements and characteristics of the targeted group(s) or segment(s) of customers. This marketing programme will aim to position the product, brand or service directly at the targeted consumers. Such positioning will take into consideration the offerings of competing organisations within the same segment.

The benefits which a market segmentation approach offers are many and varied. These benefits include a better understanding of customer needs and wants, which can lead to more carefully tuned and effective marketing programmes; greater insight into the competitive situation, which assists in the identification and maintenance of a differential advantage; and more effective resource allocation. Rarely is it realistic to target 100 per cent of a market, so focusing on certain segments allows organisations to make efficient use of their resources. For example, Apple computers initially focused its efforts on the education sector, becoming expert in this particular application.

8.4.2 The Segmentation Process

Any market segmentation consists of three distinct stages. It is important to fully understand these stages before making any major decisions about how different markets should be segmented. The illustration below demonstrates the relationship between the key stages.

Segmentation

- Consider different variables for segmenting the market than those currently used.
- Look at the profile of the emerging (new and existing) segments.
- Check the validity of the segments.

Targeting

- Decide on an appropriate targeting strategy.
- Which and how many segments should be targeted.
- Which are the priority target segments.

Positioning

- In each segment, understand customer perceptions of all key brands.
- Position the business's products in the mind of the customers and distributors/dealers in the targeted segment against rivals' products.
- Design an appropriate marketing mix which conveys this desired positioning to the targeted customers.

Put simply, the underlying principle of the three stages is that 'similar' customers can be grouped. For example, an audience of 100 managers asked about their favourite car model might give 100 different responses. However, some of the responses might refer to sports cars, others to 4-wheel drive off-road vehicles, while a further group could be centred on executive cars. In situations where such 'similar' consumers can be collected into large enough groups, there is obvious potential for companies wishing to target such *segments*.

8.4.3 *Carrying out Segmentation*

Carrying out segmentation, the stage where customers are aggregated into groups, involves two basic steps:

1. Segmentation variables (also called *base variables*) are used to group together customers who demonstrate similar product requirements. When choosing appropriate segmentation bases it is necessary to select those which clearly distinguish between different product requirements. For example, publishers of children's books may segment their customer base according to age.

Probably the most popular industrial or business to business segmentation bases include:

- Geographic location
- Type of organisation
- Trade category
- Customer size/characteristics
- Customers' business sectors
- Product-related features:
    purchase behaviour,
    purchase occasion,
    benefits sought from having the product,
    consumption behaviour,
    attitude to product/service.

A common approach is to link geographic territory with customers' industrial sector, such as with UK plant hire.

Please bear in mind that choosing segmentation bases is a fairly subjective process, so it is rarely possible to categorically assert that there is one best way to segment a particular market. However, it is essential that the variables chosen do break down customer needs in a meaningful way. For example, theoretically it might be possible to identify groups of car buyers based on hair colour, but there is no evidence that hair colour affects people's needs in this category! Therefore this would be a meaningless approach to adopt.

In consumer markets, companies used to break down customers by income, age and social class. Increasingly, consumer marketers look to additional information, such as customers' perceptions of the benefits attained from purchasing a product, their usage behaviour, and motivation. Figure 8.2 summarises popular segmentation bases in consumer markets.

Figure 8.2 *Segmentation Bases in Consumer Markets*

Basic Customer Characteristics

Owing to the ease with which such information can be obtained, the use of these variables is widespread.

- **Demographics**
  Age   Sex
  Family   Marital Status
  Race   Religion
  Family Life Cycle

- **Socio-Economics**
  Income   Occupation
  Education   Social Class

- **Geographic Location**
  Country   Region
  Type of Urban Area   Type of Housing
  Urban/Rural

- **Personality, Motives and Lifestyle**
  Consumer's Personality
  Motives for Purchasing/Consuming
  Consumer's Lifestyle and Aspirations

Product Related Behavioural Characteristics

- **Purchase Behaviour**
  Brand Loyalty versus Triggers for Switching

- **Purchase Occasion**
  Novelty   Frequency
  Event   Dealer Location

- **Benefits Sought**
  Perhaps the most popular consumer segmentation base: the benefits sought by the consumer from purchasing, consuming, having the product or service

- **Consumption Behaviour and User Status**
  Heavy users versus light and non-users

- **Attitude to Product/Service**
  Different Customers' Perceptions
  Consumers' Communication

2. Once segments have been identified using one or a combination of the base variables above, as much as possible must be done to understand the characteristics of the customers in those segments. This understanding will make it easier for the marketer to design a marketing programme which will appeal to the segment targeted. Building up a fuller picture of the segments is called *profiling* and uses *descriptor variables*. Descriptors can include variables relating to customer characteristics or product-related behavioural variables. In fact, the more extensive the picture, the better.

Sometimes people find the distinction between *base* and *descriptor variables* confusing. Just remember that *base* variables are used first to allocate customers to segments while *descriptors* help later in building up a profile of segment membership. For example, a hotel chain segmented its customer base in terms of benefits sought by customers (base variable) thus identifying a group of customers requiring luxury four-star standard rooms. Profiling these customers using descriptors showed that these were mainly business travellers, located predominantly in the south of the country.

8.4.4 *Essential Qualities for Effective Segments*

As has been stated, there is rarely one 'right' way to segment a market, but there are some criteria which can help to decide on the robustness of a particular approach. Before implementing a segmentation scheme, check that the segments satisfy the following conditions:

- *Measurable*: it must be possible to delimit, measure and assess the segments for market potential.
- *Substantial*: in order to warrant marketing activity, the identified segment must be large enough to be viable and therefore worthwhile targeting with products/services. Separate businesses will have different views as to viable size: Toyota versus Morgan Cars, for example.
- *Accessible*: having identified a market segment, and checked its potential viability, the marketer must be able to action a marketing programme with a finely developed marketing mix for targeted customers. Sometimes the similarities between customers are not sufficient to implement full marketing programmes.
- *Stable*: there must be an assessment of a segment's short, medium and long term viability, particularly in the light of competitor and marketing environment changes. Segments rarely remain the same

over time, so it is necessary to weigh up the extent and impact of likely changes.

8.5 **Targeting**

Once segments have been identified, decisions about how many and which customer groups to target must be made. The options include:

- *Mass marketing strategy*: offering one product concept to most of the market, across many market segments. Although scale economies can be achieved, there is the risk that few customers will be adequately satisfied.
- *Single segment strategy*: concentrating on a single segment with one product concept. This is relatively cheap in resources, but very risky if the segment should fail.
- *Multi-segment strategy*: targeting a different product concept at each of a number of segments. Although this approach can spread the risk of being over committed in one area, it can be extremely resource hungry. This is the most common approach in most businesses, but within a specific profit centre it would normally be better to focus on just one or two segments. Entries into other areas could be undertaken on an *ad hoc* basis, typically to support other profit centre marketing approaches.

Which target market strategy a company adopts will depend on a host of market, product and competitive factors. Each of these must be carefully considered before a decision is made about segments to be targeted. Before making a commitment to any segment it is essential to consider the following issues:

- *Existing market share/market homogeneity.* How similar is the market to current areas of activity and does the business have market share or brand awareness in related areas on which it can build? For example, Elida Gibbs is in a strong position to target a new segment of shampoo users, because it already has considerable credibility in this area.
- *Product homogeneity.* Does the business have relevant expertise on which to build in a related product field, with associated economies of scope? A company developing computer based manufacturing systems will have expertise which is transferable across a number of industries.
- *Nature of competitive environment.* What is the level of competition

in the market and how is this changing over time? For example, the dominance of Nintendo and Sega in the computer games market makes certain segments unattractive to potential competitors.

- *Customer needs.* How extreme/easy to satisfy are customer requirements? Businesses producing highly technical, bespoke software solutions may choose not to follow up particular opportunities.
- *Segment size, structure and future potential.* How big is the segment or market, how is it made up and how is it likely to develop in the future? How will aspects of the marketing environment (see Figure 3.2) impact on sales potential? The environmental movement has caused a massive expansion to certain markets and a dampening effect in others.
- *Company resources.* Does the business have the resources to target the segment under consideration? Inevitably, there will be tough decisions to make in terms of how resources are allocated among existing and new segments.

Taking a balanced view of these factors helps companies make decisions about the viability of particular segments and ensures that resources are appropriately targeted.

The DPM (directional policy matrix described in Chapter 7: 7.2) can assist in identifying attractive markets in which the business has strengths for prioritising target segments. Each segment should be rated in terms of market attractiveness and business position, then located on a DPM grid as in Figure 7.2. Those segments towards the centre and top left of the grid should be target segment priorities (see Figure 7.3).

Figure 8.3, which uses the UK car market as an example, provides a summary for the determination of target markets.

Figure 8.3 **Determination of Target Markets**

Market Segment Name (list in order of priority)	Characteristics of Market	Criteria: Reasons for Selecting as a Target Priority?	Existing Product/Service Offered

- List target markets in order of importance (rank)
- State why each market is important
- Summarise the products offered to each market

8.6 **Summary**

This chapter has reviewed the business mission and the first two components of marketing strategy: market segmentation and target market selection. Using the business mission as a guide, the market's segments may have been revised. In addition, the business's choice of which segments – or customer groupings – it wishes to prioritise as targets will have been updated.

9

Basis for Competing: Differential Advantage and Brand or Product Positioning

9.1 Introduction

Once the target segments have been identified, the business must determine the basis on which it is to compete in the selected markets. How to position the brand within the minds of the targeted customers must also be appraised. The purpose of this chapter is to review these marketing strategy issues and provide an approach for recording the necessary decisions.

9.2 Basis for Competing: Why Important?

A basis for competing hinges on successfully identifying a differential advantage (DA) or competitive edge. Without one, success in the marketplace is difficult over the longer term and the business will be highly vulnerable to competitors' moves. Businesses in this position may be forced to trade purely on the basis of price, and in such circumstances any company eventually struggles. With a differential advantage, marketing programmes can emphasise the unique strength or advantage. Competitors are put in the awkward position of having to catch up, before they can even contemplate getting ahead.

A differential advantage – or competitive edge – is something the business has, or one of its products has, *which is highly desired by the target market* and is not currently readily matched by rival companies or products. It can be based around a wide variety of issues, including technical competence, service, delivery, breadth of product range, etc.

Rover in press advertisements stresses the capabilities and friendliness of its dealers; Chanel the eminence of its brands and fragrances; the AA its coverage and ability to help; 3M its innovative creativity; DHL its speed and reliability; Duracell the longevity of its cells; BA's new Club World the added service, comfort and convenience; JCB the reassurance in its brand.

9.2.1 Steps in Determining a Differential Advantage

The following steps can help businesses identify and secure a differential advantage:

1. Identify the market's segments.

2. Determine what product and service attributes are desired and demanded by each segment or customer group.

3. Establish which of these attributes the business offers.

4. Determine the business's competitors' offers. For example, what are their genuine strengths (as perceived by the marketplace)?

5. Establish where there are gaps between customer expectations and competitors' offers.

6. Find out whether any of these gaps are matched by the business and its products or services. If so, these are differential advantages (DAs).

7. Determine whether the business can emphasise any of these advantages through sales and marketing programmes.

8. Question how sustainable are these advantages for the business. For example, how easily can competitors catch up and how well can the business defend these advantages?

9. If there are no current advantages for the business, given the gaps identified between competitors' offerings and customer expectations, identify what the business must do to try and rectify the situation.

10. In order to maximise any existing or potential advantages, decide what changes the business must make to its R&D, engineering, sales and marketing.

9.2.2 Givens Versus Advantages

Managers often identify apparent advantages which are no more than just strengths. Competitive prices, consistent quality, technical performance, delivery, brand credibility, technical support may be keen, but in reality may be matched – if not bettered – by at least some of the strongest competitors. A strength is not a differential advantage or competitive edge if matched by rivals. For example, a pharmaceutical company which is first in the race to produce a new form of drug has a differential advantage, but only until competitors catch up and patents lapse.

Similarly, an advantage or strength is not really the basis for competing in a market if in reality it is a 'given' – something expected and taken for granted by customers and dealers. Keen price, delivery on time, product quality are just some examples of attributes customers assume to be there and which are taken for granted. A differential advantage has to go further; it must genuinely appeal to customers and be ahead of the competition's offer.

In 1993, a workshop for a leading manufacturer of paints identified these bases for competing differential advantages. Subsequent work showed these attributes to be 'givens' – aspects either taken for granted by customers or matched by rivals:

- Competitive price
- Consistent quality
- Technical performance
- Delivery
- Credibility
- Technical support

The determination of a real differential advantage proved harder to describe, but was eventually summed up by various points which together gave this statement of differential or competitive advantage:

> We start with *technical innovation* which we can *manufacture* and *supply globally*, backed up by *local* teams with a high level of *expertise* in *technical service*, supported by a *wide product range*. Finally, being part of a large corporation gives added credibility.

> Strong global presence – being able to talk to customers world-wide at all levels.

9.2.3 Assessing Differential Advantages

For each segment determine what product/service/marketing/brand attributes are required or expected by these customers and dealers. Decide which of these attributes is (or could be) offered by the business. Determine whether any of these attributes are offered by any leading competitors. If they are not, they may form the basis for a differential advantage or competitive edge for the business. These attributes wanted by target customers, provided by the business and not matched by leading rivals, must be capable of seeming attractive to distributors and to customers; they must be suitable to form the core of sales and marketing programmes, otherwise they are not really the basis for competing. Figure 9.1 provides a suitable summary for this analysis. The example is based on the UK car market.

Figure 9.1 Identification of DAs

Example: Car Market

Segment Name	Identified Advantages (Strengths) for the Business Over Rivals	Are Advantages Sufficient Basis for a DA (Differential Advantage)?
1 Fleet	• Range of models • Dealer network • Volume discounts	No No No
2 Private (Family)	• Safety features • Local dealer • Value	Possible Possible No
3 Executive	• Model range • Innovative features • Brand image	No Possible Yes
4 Private (Single)	• Niche model • Image • Value	Yes Yes No
5		
6		
7		
8		

• Record any DAs held by the business over rivals
• Remember a strength is only a possible DA if target customers desire it and rivals do not offer it
• To qualify as a DA, the strength must be cost effective and in the short term, defensible

9.3 Brand and Product Positionings

9.3.1 The Importance of Positioning

Brand and product positioning hinges upon customer perceptions of how one offering compares with others in the marketplace. Managers' views are important, but there is no substitute for identifying how **customers** and **distributors** perceive brands and products in comparison with the strengths of competitors' offers. Before any marketing strategy can be determined or brand positioning strategy implemented it is essential that the market's perceptions are known.

9.3.2 The Positioning Map

Perceptual mapping is based on a variety of mathematical and qualitative approaches designed to place or describe consumers' perceptions of brands or products on one or a series of 'spatial maps'. It is a means of visually depicting consumers' perceptions, showing the relative positionings of different brands or products (and thereby companies).

The core attributes should be identified through qualitative consumer research, with follow-up confirmatory research identifying the relative positionings of the brands or companies to be plotted. For example, a perceptual map of the UK furniture market, as produced in the late 1980s, identified 'value for money' as the key attribute. Research showed that consumers were in reality more concerned with price and specifically product quality.

It is important for all marketers to understand the positioning of their products on such a spatial map, *vis-à-vis* competitors, particularly in order to develop realistic and effective marketing programmes. Figure 9.2 presents a completed example for the European car industry. Marketing research identified the variables and the positions. If more than two variables are thought to be critical, several positioning maps may be constructed. Software programs exist which plot three or more variables on three-dimensional maps, but in most instances, simple two-dimensional maps as shown in Figure 9.2 are sufficient.

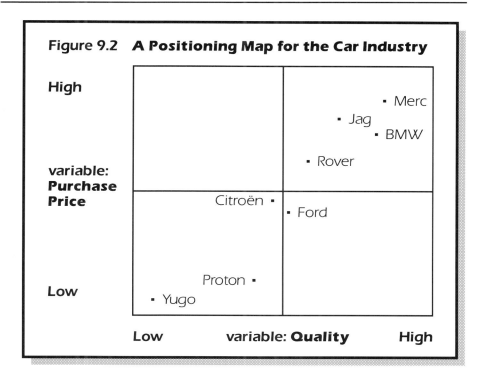

Figure 9.2 **A Positioning Map for the Car Industry**

9.3.3 Producing the Positioning Map

The analyses so far undertaken (see Figures 2.1, 5.3 and 6.2) have ascertained the core Key Customer Values desired or demanded by customers. This work has presented a listing or league table of these KCVs. The positioning map should use these leading KCVs as the variables for the X- and Y-axes on one or more perceptual maps. The business's product positions should be marked on the map – or graph – along with the positions for all leading competitors – direct and substitutes. The relative distances between the companies indicates their ability or inability to satisfactorily match customers' needs for the main KCVs. Figure 9.3 presents a blueprint positioning map.

Figure 9.3 *The Positioning Map*

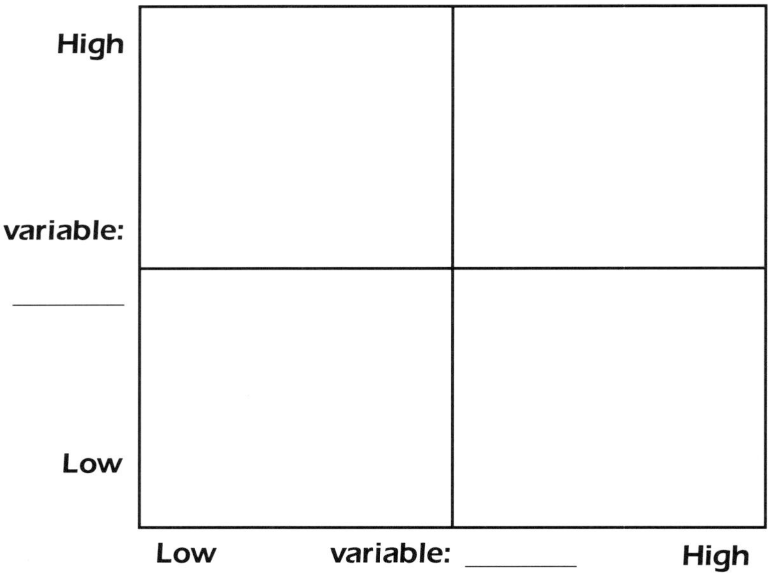

High

variable:

_____

Low

Low   variable: _____   High

- Let customer feedback specify the KCVs to use on the map's axes
- Plot customers' perceptions of the relative positionings (locations) on the map of the business's and leading competitors' brands or products

9.4 *Strategy Recommendations*

The previous sections in this chapter, also Chapter 8, have outlined the requirements for determining an updated marketing strategy. The business must have very clear and specific recommendations in terms of basis for competing and desired brand positioning. The purpose of this section is to crystallise these recommendations to ensure there are no ambiguous statements which can be misinterpreted within the marketing function and in the other functional areas of the business.

9.4.1 Changing Strategies

The background analyses (Chapter 2) have highlighted the strengths and weaknesses implicit in the current view of core target markets, and the need to update key customer targets. The additional analyses (Chapters 3 to 7, plus 8) have brought together a depth of information relating to the market and its current characteristics: customer needs and expectations; general market trends and impacting aspects of the external marketing environment; competitive positions and competitors' strengths; basis for competing and differential advantage; brand or product positionings; and strengths, weaknesses, opportunities and threats.

In the light of this information, strategy decisions have now been made (Figure 9.4):

- Which groups of customers to target
- With what positioning or offer
- On what competitive basis

9.4.2 The Need for a Differential Advantage

All organisations strive to attain or develop a differential advantage for their products or services: a feature perceived by target customers to be

a) highly desirable, and

b) not offered by rival companies.

Most organisations fail to determine such an advantage, but those which do clearly have an advantage in their markets. As section 9.2 has outlined, it is essential for the business to seek a differential advantage or competitive edge for each of its products or services. For example, Volvo has built its differential advantage on safety, Fairy washing-up liquid on its long lasting qualities. Where a DA is identified, it must be stressed in all associated sales and marketing programmes and in the positioning strategy. Often positioning statements (or straplines) are used to emphasise this positioning. For example, Kellogg's claims to be the 'original and best to you' each morning.

9.4.3 Required Positioning

With the aid of a positioning map (see Figures 9.2 and 9.3), explain for each target segment the required product or brand positioning *vis-à-vis* the key competitors along the key customer values (KCVs) identified in Figures 2.1 and 5.3. Remember, these dimensions must be seen as important by the customers not just by the business's own executives.

This is a fundamental step in the determination of the strategy. The stated required positioning must:

- be based on customers' identified needs;
- take into account competitors' positionings and their ability to deliver to these customer needs;
- maximise any identified differential advantage; and
- feed into sales and marketing programmes.

One of the principal aims of the eventual marketing programmes, as discussed in Section IV, must be to offer products and service which deliver this desired product positioning to the targeted customers, with programmes which communicate the proposition to these target customers.

9.5 Summarising Strategy Decisions

In the light of the core analyses so far undertaken, it is helpful to summarise the following key strategy decisions:

a) Which core markets are to be targeted? Why these?

b) What are the required product positioning strategies? Why these?

c) What are the fundamental differential advantages?

d) What should be the priorities for the business?

Summarise these key strategic decisions in Figure 9.4. A sample copy of this chart has been completed for illustration using the UK car market as an example.

Figure 9.4 **Target Marketing Strategy Summary Statement**

Example: car market 'executive' segment

Core Targeted Segments/Markets						
Segment	**1:**	**2:**	**3:** *Executive*	**4:**	**5:**	**6:**
Principal Reason for Segment Being Target Priority			*Stability* *Value* *History*			
Likely Sales Current Year (units)			*1,300 units*			
Likely Sales Next Year			*1,600 units*			
KCVs per Segment			• *Image* • *Performance* • *Reliability* • *Safety*			
Required Brand Positioning			• *Innovative* • *Quality*			
Main Two Competitors			*BMW* *Mercedes*			
Principal Competitive Threat			*Competitors' model launches* *Rivals' dealer networks*			
Differential Advantage (DA)			*Brand image*			
Key Problems to Overcome			*Brand Image* *Feature level* *Performance* *Dealer network*			
Capital Implications from Strategy			*Advertising Budget* *Product Development* *Distribution Network*			

• This is the overall statement of target market strategy and must be fully completed

9.6 Summary

Within each target market, the business should have evaluated its competitive edge against its rivals to determine any differential advantage or, at worst, the strengths it will be best placed to emphasise in its marketing programmes. In each priority market segment, there should be a clear recommendation for how the business's products and brands should be pitched against its rivals. This positioning strategy must be implemented and communicated through the marketing plan's recommended marketing programmes, outlined in Section IV of this workbook. Finally, the key marketing strategy information has been summarised.

10

Marketing Objectives and Gap Analysis

10.1 Introduction

Marketing objectives are an essential part of the marketing plan, giving a sense of direction to the specified marketing programmes of Section IV. Without such objectives it would be difficult to judge exactly what the marketing plan is trying to achieve, when, or whether it has been successful! Gap analysis examines recent variations between forecasts for sales volumes or profitability and the actual achieved figures, illustrating the scale of the marketing task in hand. It is a useful technique for ensuring over-ambitious goals are tempered and for encouraging lagging colleagues to think ahead with a desire for new ideas and plans.

This chapter gives guidance on determining marketing objectives and shows how this task is linked to the analyses already undertaken. The steps required in Gap analysis are then reviewed with supporting charts to be completed.

10.2 Marketing Objectives

Key marketing objectives to achieve the recommended strategy must be determined by referring back to the earlier analyses to ensure that the objectives make sense in terms of market trends and are consistent with strengths, weaknesses and the competitive situation. The resulting marketing objectives must be designed to implement the target market strategy as summarised in Figure 9.4.

Do not be surprised if some objectives are broad while others are quite specific. Figure 10.1 has been designed to cope with these differences by asking first for general objectives and then for a more detailed target segment by segment view. Start with the general strategic objectives (try to limit these to between six and eight) then move onto the more specific target market objectives. For example, a European car manufacturer might have the following general objectives: to increase market share from X to Y per cent, to launch two new products, to win first time buyers and to expand market demand. The same manufacturer might identify the following specific target market objectives: to

Figure 10.1 **Marketing Objectives**

General Strategic Marketing Objectives	
•	
•	
•	
•	
•	
•	
Segment:	**Objective:**
Segment:	**Objective:**
Segment:	**Objective:**
Segment:	**Objective:**
Segment:	**Objective:**
Segment:	**Objective:**

- First list overall marketing objectives
- Indicate the most important differences for leading target markets
- Include a time scale for each objective

convert customers from rival manufacturer X, to convert current customers from an old model and to attract first time buyers.

Remember that marketing objectives should be expressed in terms of products/services and markets and must be capable of measurement. This means the objectives should focus on a combination of the following:

- Existing products or services in existing markets
- New products or services for existing markets
- Existing products or services for new markets
- New products or services for new markets.

These objectives need describing in terms of values, volumes and market shares and should have a clearly defined time scale. These details will help to refine subsequent marketing programmes for implementation (Section IV).

10.3 Gap Analysis

0.3.1 The Nature of Gap Analysis

In marketing terms, the *gap* is the difference between a product's (or market's) actual performance and its predicted performance, usually in terms of return on investment, cash generation or use, return on sales and market share. In this instance, the business should focus on projected sales volumes versus actual sales, of principal product groups and leading individual lines. *Gap analysis* is the process of determining the gaps between actual and predicted sales, diagnosing reasons for any discrepancy and outlining required corrective action.

Where there is an unfavourable gap – instances where actual sales are not as high as hoped for – which is commonly the case, there are several options in terms of corrective action for the business to follow:

- Improved productivity: reduced costs, improved sales mix, higher prices.
- Market penetration: increased rate of usage, increased market share.
- Market extension: new user groups, enter new segments, geographical expansion.
- Product development: new products, new features, modified products, revised ranges.
- Diversification: new products sold to new markets.

The first two options are operational issues, requiring greater effort and clearer use of existing products and working practices. The remaining three options are more strategic, necessitating alterations to the company's strategy.

10.3.2 The Gap Analysis Process

Gap analysis helps to decide how to move forward to where strategic goals say the organisation needs to be.

1. The first step is to plot *recent* (e.g. for the last two or three years) and *current* actual turnover or volume sales achievements on the gap analysis graph: Figure 10.2. For those requiring it, Appendix A1 presents more detailed guidance for forecasting.

2. The second step is to plot the sales forecasts for this *same period.*

Already there will be a gap revealed for the past few years between actual and forecast performance.

3. In the third step, plot current predictions/projections for the *next few years.* These forecasts should be as realistic as possible and made on the basis of no change to the company's current strategy: i.e. where the business would be if it continued as previously and simply maintained the *status quo.*

Expectations must be realistic – sometimes marketing plans fail because those preparing them set targets which are not achievable.

4. Finally, extrapolate the actual sales line from known current sales, on the graph for the same period as the forecasts made in step three.

There inevitably will be a gap already apparent in the trends revealed for the next few years by the two lines graphed in stages three and four.

The space between the two lines – actual/extrapolated and predicted figures – over the next few years represents the *gap* which marketing programmes must fill if the new targets are to be achieved.

For those requiring it, Appendix A1 presents more detailed guidance for forecasting.

Figure 10.2 The Gap Chart

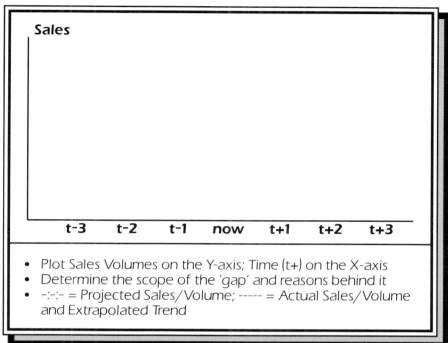

- Plot Sales Volumes on the Y-axis; Time (t+) on the X-axis
- Determine the scope of the 'gap' and reasons behind it
- -:-:- = Projected Sales/Volume; ----- = Actual Sales/Volume and Extrapolated Trend

0.3.3 Gap Analysis: Corrective Action Required

The space between the two lines – actual and predicted figures – over the past few years and for the next few years represents the *gap* which marketing programmes must aim to address if the targets are to be achieved. The detailed actions recommended by the marketing plans must either:

a) modify sales forecasts, or

b) produce marketing programmes capable of filling the gap; that is: designed to boost sales significantly to reduce the gap.

It is worth questioning what market and internal factors have led to recent forecasts not being achieved. Were the resultant gaps perhaps avoidable if forecasts had been more enlightened? Could action have been taken to address the gaps? Should lessons be learnt and applied to current forecasting? For example, a country which has recently become politically unstable is likely to attract a lower level of foreign investment than might otherwise have been expected.

Consideration must also be given to the current product life cycle stage (infancy, growth, maturity, decline) and to the competitive position, to ensure that recommendations reflect competitors' actions/ strengths and the inherent ability of the products to achieve required forecast sales.

Realising there are deficiencies between current actual sales and

Figure 10.3 Corrective Actions Required to Close the Gap

Corrective Action 1: Productivity	
Better product mix	Description?
More sales calls	Such as? To whom?
Better sales calls	In what manner?
Cost reduction	How?
Increase price	To what? With what implications?
Reduced discounts	Of what? To whom? When?
Improved asset utilisation	Such as?
Other: _____	
Other: _____	

Figure 10.3 (continued)

Corrective Action 2: Ansoff's Strategic Options		

PRODUCT

	Present	New
Present	Market Penetration Possibilities: • • • •	Product Development Requirements: • • • •
New	Market Development Opportunities: • • • •	Diversification: • • • •

MARKET (row label between Present and New)

- Consider the options available in closing the gap
- State what corrective action is now required or possible
- Be as detailed/specific as possible
- Be realistic: do not present over-extensive lists

forecast sales, and that there is – as a result of this analysis – the expectation that there will continue to be a gap if the existing *status quo* remains, consider what corrective action is required. The options include a boost in terms of marketing productivity, or in terms of product and market developments. Use Figure 10.3 to outline what must be done.

Remember that the resulting marketing mix programmes in the marketing plan must aim to achieve these strategic recommendations, but must also be capable of doing so. It is essential to be focused rather than over-ambitious.

10.4 Summary

The Gap analysis should have shown for the recent past how close to forecast financial sales targets the business has been. Reasons for significant gaps must be examined in order to make this plan's recommendations more realistic. The marketing plan's marketing objectives must be clear, building on from the stated marketing strategy now determined (see Figure 9.4). The marketing objectives need to determine whether the business's thrust and required products are focusing on existing markets with current or new products and services, or new markets with current or new products and services.

Section III Checklist

By the end of this *Marketing Strategy Summary* section of *The Marketing Planning Workbook* you should have:
- Revisited the business's mission statement
- Determined the priority target markets
- Assessed a basis for competing
- Produced a desired brand positioning strategy
- Listed the essential marketing objectives
- Developed a Gap analysis with recommendations for closing the gap

These are the most important aspects of marketing strategy within marketing planning. These strategic decisions cannot be determined until the marketing analyses outlined in Section II have been undertaken. Until these strategic recommendations are finalised it is foolhardy to develop the marketing plan's implementation programmes, described in Section IV.

The Marketing Planning Workbook

Section I
Perspective

Section II
Core Analyses

Section III
Analyses into Strategy

Section IV
Programmes for Implementation

Section V
The Marketing Plan Document

Section IV

Programmes for Implementation

Analyses need to be translated into actions. Programmes have to be created to implement the stated target market and positioning strategies, maximising identified marketing opportunities and differential advantages. Resources, personnel, budgets and time frames must be allocated to these tasks. Consideration should be given to longer term requirements and to monitoring the effectiveness of the marketing plans. Section IV details the requirements for programmes to implement the marketing plan's strategic recommendations. There is also guidance offered for setting up a marketing planning programme and on how to manage the associated people and cultural issues within the business.

- Actions – marketing programmes – required to implement target market strategies and the marketing plans
- Allocation of responsibilities, resources, budgets and schedules
- Ramifications for other areas of the business
- On-going work requirements
- Assessing progress
- Managing a marketing planning programme – people and cultural issues

11

Required Marketing Programmes

11.1 Introduction

The marketing strategy determined in Section III will not be actioned unless a deliberate set of activities is put in place to implement the desired strategy. Marketing programmes must be designed which reflect the requirements of the strategy and which aim to satisfy targeted customers' needs. These marketing programmes hinge on the *marketing mix* ingredients: the product (or service) offering, promotional campaigns, place/distribution/channel requirements, pricing levels/policies and people/customer service issues.

The marketing programmes must match the aims of the specified target market strategy. In addition, they must reflect the market situation and company position as outlined in the marketing analyses described in Section II of this workbook. The marketing programmes also must aim to deliver the necessary customer needs (KCVs), emphasise any identified differential advantage (DA) held by the business, and intend to alter customers' perceptions in order to achieve the desired stated brand positioning for the business's products.

In the light of the analyses undertaken in Section II and the requirements of the strategy determined in Section III, it is important to remember that it is highly unlikely existing sales and marketing programmes will be adequate or relevant. There will need to be significant modifications and enhancements. This chapter examines the nature of the required marketing programmes, leading to the detailed identification of the required marketing mix actions.

11.2 Issues to Emphasise

There are some core issues which need to be stressed during the development of the marketing mix programmes: key customer values (KCVs), competitive threats, any differential advantage over rivals, desired positioning. Use Figure 11.1 to summarise these issues so that they are not inadvertently ignored while the marketing mix programmes are developed. Remember, the marketing programmes *must* be developed with the intention of satisfying customers, matching or beating competitors' moves, while emphasising any strengths or differential advantages with a view to achieving the

Figure 11.1 Summary by Segment of KCVs and DAs

Example: earthmoving equipment market

	Segment 1: *Large civil engineers*	Segment 2:	Segment 3:	Segment 4:	Segment 5:	Segment 6:
CAT						
Summary of KCVs	*Performance Reliability 'Local' support*					
Main Competitive Threat to the Company	*Komatsu initial price*					
Any company DA? What?	*Economies of scale Dealer network Logistics system*					
Desired positioning	*Innovative, reliable, robust product*					

desired positioning. The copy of Figure 11.1 shown uses information from the global earthmoving equipment market.

11.3 The Marketing Mix

The marketing mix is the set of tactical decisions made by marketers which determines the specific marketing actions taken in the market-place by a business. These ingredients must be manipulated in a manner which ensures targeted customers are satisfied, marketing strategies are implemented and desired brand positioning is achieved. In this context, such decisions about the marketing activity required must be direct, clear and realistic. It is likely that a separate marketing mix approach will be required for each individual target market or market segment.

Given the importance of determining the appropriate marketing mix programmes, this book establishes the requirements and dimensions of each ingredient of the marketing mix. This is particularly important in a marketing planning context as the detailed marketing mix recommendations form the visible output from the programme and are at the heart of the marketing plan document.

The marketing mix is the tool kit of any marketing department, consisting principally of the '5 Ps': Product (or Service), Promotion, Place (Distribution/Channels to Market), Pricing and People. Owing to differing customer characteristics and buying behaviour, each target market requires a bespoke marketing mix or set of marketing programmes.

This section presents twelve summary forms which highlight the principal aspects of the marketing mix programme recommendations. These will form the specified direct actions at the core of the final marketing plan:

11.2   Customer Perceptions: Need for Change

11.3   Summary of Required Product/Service Mix

11.4   Required Service Levels to Support Product Mix

11.5   Summary of Current Advertising and Promotion

11.6   Key Promotional Activity Required

11.7   Desired Promotional Programmes

11.8   Distribution Channel Structural Requirements

11.9   Summary of Marketing Channel Structural Requirements

11.10 Sales Links Through Suppliers/Contractors

11.11 Summary of Pricing Policy and Pricing Levels

11.12 Process/Customer Liaison Improvements Required

11.13 Human Resource Requirements

In order to understand current areas of weakness, it is important initially to identify *perceptions* in the target markets of certain fundamental marketing attributes, including brand awareness; product awareness; product image; quality of deliverable/product; after sales liaison/support and technical expertise; value of deliverable/product; product performance; on-time delivery and service professionalism versus the main competitors. Figure 11.2, which identifies desirable improvements which can be made by modifying the business's marketing programmes, provides a simple summary chart for this information.

Figure 11.2   Customer Perceptions: the Need for Change - The Business vs Leading Rivals

	Current Perceptions:				
	Positive		Neutral	Negative	
	++	+	+/−	−	− −
Brand Awareness					
Product Awareness					
Product/Brand Image					
Quality of Product/ Deliverable					
After Sales Liaison/Support					
Value of Product/ Deliverable					
Product Performance					
On-Time Delivery					
Service Professionalism					
Technical Expertise					
Other:					
Other:					
Other:					

NB: Competitor 1 is: **Competitor 2 is:**

- Produce one form per targeted segment
- First enter the business's rating: ++, +, +/−, − or − −. NB: ++ = very positive/good; +/− = neutral; − − = highly negative/very poor
- Second enter the ratings for the two leading rivals in the segment
- Use this coding to mark companies on the chart: B = the business; 1 = main rival; 2 = second main rival. Name these competitors on the figure

In the context of these perceptions and standing versus leading rivals, on which features must the business work immediately?

1.3.1 Products

A *product* is everything (both favourable and unfavourable) that a customer receives in an exchange; it is a complexity of tangible and intangible attributes, including functional, social and psychological utilities or benefits. A product may be a good, a service or an idea. The *product mix* is the composite selection of products which a business makes available to its customers.

There are three *levels* of a product to consider: the core product, actual product and augmented product. The core product is the benefit or service recognised and desired by the target customer. The actual product is a composite of 'real' attributes, including product features, quality, capabilities, design/styling, packaging and brand name. The augmented product aspects are the 'softer', service-orientated issues which help ease the purchase and use of a product and reassure customers, such as warranty provision, customer service, delivery and credit, installation, after-sales support and involvement of personnel. For example, when a family purchases a system for playing computer games, the core benefit will be the entertainment which the system provides. The actual product will be made up of the system's brand name, style, packaging and technical specification. In addition, the family will expect a level of customer service, in terms of after-sales support and warranty back-up, should problems be encountered with the system (augmented product).

Businesses must ensure they have the correct mix of products guaranteed to appeal to target markets and satisfy these customers. This will involve the continuation of some (or all) of existing products, the modification or deletion of others in the product portfolio, and perhaps the development of new products. If a product must be dropped, there are three options: an immediate withdrawal, a run out or a phased course of action. The product life cycle analysis is an important consideration, as a successful company must have a balance of products, with rapidly growing and mature products providing the support for the development and nurturing of new products. Dependency on mature and declining products clearly is a recipe for disaster.

Having a correct and appropriate product mix is essential to the success of any business. Any changes deemed necessary must be incorporated in the product recommendations resulting from the marketing planning process. These requirements are not just in terms of the actual product, but also for the overall augmented product offering, including aspects of customer service, handling and reassurance. The selected product mix must reflect the identified KCVs.

Figure 11.3 **Summary of Required Product/Service Mix**

Example: UK truck market

Segment/ Market *UK truck market*	Title of the Business's Relevant Product or Service	Product or Service Description
1 *New Purchasers*	*Warranty plus*	*Option of extended warranty*
2 *Existing users*	*Exchange units*	*Parts exchange programme*
3 *Competitive users*	*Multi part*	*Range of competitively priced parts for competitors' trucks*
4		

- List out existing products/services pertinent to each target segment's needs and KCVs
- Column 2 = popular name/acronym within the business; column 3 = the common usage description meaningful to the customers

Segment/ Market	Additional Product/Service Requirements	Product/Service Attributes	Rationale
Small Business	*Hire purchase finance*	*Low rates Simple paperwork*	*Match competitors*
Large haulage firms	*Biodegradeable lubes*	*Environmentally friendly oils/ lubricants*	*Marketing environment trend*

- In this section, detail any new/additional products needed in the light of the marketing analyses to maintain the business's competitive position or facilitate the business's target market strategy
- Note, the 'new product' could be a hybrid of activities which cuts across the business's divisions/departments/sectors

Figure 11.4 Required Service Levels to Support Product Mix

Example: UK truck market

	Segment 1:	Segment 2:	Segment 3:	Segment 4:
		Truck Exchange Units to existing users		
People		*Product knowledge* *Technical competence*		
Advice/ Guidance (not consultancy)		*Product catalogues* *Service instructions*		
On-Going Support		*Computerised stock list* *Instant ordering system* *24 hour delivery*		
Facilities		*Dealer depots* *Delivery vans* *Storage facilities*		
Other:		*Warranty terms* *Open account*		
Other:				

Any Training Requirements?
   Regular technical training
   Customer care programme
   Sales skills essential

Resource Implications
   Dealers need to invest in:
   • *Stock*
   • *Systems (computer link)*
   • *Training*
   • *Delivery vans*

- This table requests information concerning service aspects of the product offer. The products *per se* (their tangible attributes) are detailed in Figure 11.3
- Some service aspects will require retraining/orientation of personnel interfacing with customers
- These 'soft' issues connected with the product offering – such as warranties, technical advice, consumer finance, parts availability, etc.– inevitably will require resourcing

Products: required action

The required *Product/Service Mix* must be specified per target market, particularly if additional products or derivatives are required. Figure 11.3 offers a format for summarising this information and uses a European truck manufacturer as an example. It is also important to determine the required *Service Levels* necessary to support this product mix, as shown in Figures 11.4 and 11.12.

11.3.2 Promotion

Advertising is perhaps the most visible component of promotion and is viewed by many lay observers as the essence of marketing. While it may be true that for many marketers this is a major use of available budgets, there is much more to effective promotions than just advertising.

In the marketing context, *promotion* is about communicating with individuals, groups or organisations to directly or indirectly facilitate exchanges of products, services or ideas by influencing audience members to accept a business's product offering. The *promotional mix* is formed from the core promotional activities, namely advertising, direct mail, sales promotion, personal selling, public relations and sponsorship. A *target audience* is a group of consumers or target market at whom a specific promotional campaign is directly aimed, or channel members in the distribution chain.

For consumers to become customers they must adopt (buy) the business's product. The product adoption process holds that customers first must become aware of a product, must then show interest in it, be persuaded to evaluate the product, try it, before – if having evaluated and tried it they like it – adopting the product by purchasing it and using it. Different forms of promotional activity are required to facilitate each stage of the product adoption process:

■ Awareness: mass media communication sources – television, press, magazines, radio.
■ Interest: mass media communication sources – press, magazines, television, radio.
■ Evaluation: personal sources – relatives, friends, colleagues, peers.
■ Trial: personal sources – sales personnel, peers, family, friends.
■ Adoption: personal sources (sales personnel) and for re-assurance, mass media sources (television or press advertising).

For example, the purchase of a washing machine might at the awareness and interest stages involve the customers consulting local newspapers for retailer advertisements. Later on, a choice of stores may be visited and the advice of friends and relatives sought. Before a choice is made, sales personnel may be consulted about prices and servicing arrangements.

Of course, not all customers engaging in a particular purchase will have the same level of awareness and understanding of a product. This is reflected in the identification of five communications effects. Depending on what effect is required, different promotional activity will be needed. The promotional effects are:

- Category need: customers must recognise that a market exists, with specific products. They must also accept they have a need for such products.
- Brand awareness: once 'in the market', customers typically have several suppliers' brands from which to choose. A business's marketers must concentrate promotional effort on enforcing specific brand awareness of their products.
- Brand attitude: awareness is important, but targeted customers must be persuaded to have a favourable attitude to the business's brand versus competitors' brands.
- Brand purchase intention: the favourable brand attitude must be stimulated to encourage consumers to experience the product and consider making a purchase.
- Purchase facilitation: having created a recognised need for a product, brand awareness, favourable brand attitude and encouraging targeted customers to try the product through effective promotional work, the other ingredients of the marketing mix must be in harmony to make the product available at the right place, price and with the right product attributes and service levels.

Businesses using an appropriate mix of promotional elements can make the product adoption process smoother and facilitate communications effects. But before the promotional tools are selected it is important to realise that a schedule of activity must be followed:

1. Determine the target audience (target market).

2. Ascertain the key customer values and brand perceptions of the target audience.

3. Determine the business's desired brand positioning in the target market.

4. Produce a promotional message which reflects the product, brand positioning and customers' expectations.

5. Determine the timetabling required for promotional work in terms of marketing strategy requirements, competitive activity and the requirements of the rest of the marketing mix.

6. Select the most pertinent promotional tools in the context of the product, its target market, customers' behaviour and attitudes and available budgets.

7. Identify the most appropriate media channels and formats to convey the determined campaign message.

8. Produce the required promotional material and run the campaign(s).

It is essential for businesses to recognise the target audience's needs and expectations and the importance of establishing the desired brand positioning as selected by the business, *before* selecting promotional tools and media.

Note also that the target audience may not be the end-user, the ultimate consumer. The target audience may well be channel intermediaries and third parties such as wholesalers, retailers, distributors and agents. Depending on which point in the distribution channel is being targeted, a different promotional policy will be required. A *push* policy aims at the immediate channel member (e.g. manufacturer to wholesaler), whereas a *pull* policy aims promotional activity directly at the ultimate consumer (e.g. manufacturer to householder). For most businesses, there is a need to instigate both push and pull strategies, with different promotional work geared at channel members and consumers.

The promotional mix

The promotional mix consists of the following components:

- Advertising, print or broadcast: the most common forms available to businesses are press (national, local, consumer and trade), television, radio, cinema and outdoor (billboards, public transport). Advertising has many uses, including the promotion of products or organisations; to stimulate primary and selective demand; to offset competitors' advertising; to aid sales people; to increase uses and applications of a product; to remind and enforce attitudes; and, to reduce sales fluctuations.

- Direct mail: printed material designed to entice prospective custom or donors, mailed directly to customers' addresses.
- Sales promotion: activities or items which induce in intermediaries the desire to stock and sell a product, and in consumers the desire to buy a product. The most common forms include coupons, free samples, demonstrations and competitions for consumers and sales competitions, free merchandise, point-of-sale displays, trade shows and exhibitions for the trade.
- Personal selling: the process of informing and persuading customers directly through personal contact with the sales force and teleselling.
- Public relations: the planned and sustained effort of maintaining or creating good will, using press releases, feature articles, captioned photographed, press conferences, editorials, films, videos and tapes, in-company publications and newsletters, enhanced executive communications skills, VIP links, visits, seminars and meetings.
- Sponsorship: the financing or part financing of an event, personality, activity, programme or product to improve customer awareness and attain media coverage, most commonly in the arts and sports.

Promotion: action required

Promotional programmes are one of the mainstays of an organisation's sales and marketing activity. The first step is to summarise what promotional work and campaigns have been running recently (do not assume everyone who should know does!). Next, state the promotional objectives for any promotional work now needed (e.g. to build brand awareness; re-position a product against competitors; emphasise a particular application, etc). Finally, suggest suitable promotional programmes (e.g. literature, exhibitions, personal calls) and required scheduling: it is likely that a number of individuals within the organisation will have useful expertise and knowledge to contribute. So efforts to gather together the necessary expertise must be made. Figures 11.5 to 11.7 provide summary formats for this information. Figure 11.5 uses a European truck manufacturer as an illustrative example, while Figures 11.6 and 11.7 focus on the launch of a new 35mm camera from the market leader.

Remember, the promotional programmes *must* communicate the desired brand positioning to the targeted customers and emphasise any differential advantages over rivals.

Figure 11.5 **Summary of Current Advertising and Promotion**

Example: UK truck market

Nature of Campaign
What was done, when, which promotional mix elements

1. Identify characteristics of target market – competitive truck owners
2. Build database and verify contact details (24,000 prospects)
3. Direct mail campaign (3 stage)
  - *teaser mailer – Feb.*
  - *launch proposition – March*
  - *relevant product catalogues – March/April*
4. Monitor 0800 response
     Direct enquiries to local Dealer

Campaign Objectives
For example, create brand awareness; generate sales leads; counteract rival's campaign; support new product launch; etc.

Create awareness of 'multipart' products amongst competitive users.
Generate sales leads through 0800 number

Cost of Programme (if known)

Database building £96,000
Direct mail   £144,000
0800 enquiry line £60,000 pa

Results of Programme (if known)

1440 new customers opened accounts with Dealers
Turnover £720,000
Profit   £216,000

- Complete a form per targeted segment
- Note: the promotional mix includes advertising, publicity and public relations, sales promotion, personal selling, sponsorship, direct mail and literature - all forms of promotional activity

Figure 11.6 **Key Promotional Activity Required**

Example: 35mm camera market

Promotional Task	Targeted Segments							
	1 *Pros*	2 *Buffs*	3 *Advanced*	4	5	6	7	8
Build brand awareness								
Build brand image		✓	✓					
Build product awareness	✓	✓	✓					
Build product image	✓	✓						
Position against competitors	✓	✓						
Re-position against competitors								
Create primary demand for product								
Influence customers' KCVs		✓						
Generate sales leads	✓	✓						
Promote after-sales support								
Promote dealers/ distributors								
Support dealers' promotions								
Promote customer credit								
Influence customer buying process								
Other:								
Other:								

- Indicate promotional requirements per targeted segment
- Keep selections to the bare minimum – too many will not be feasible or cost effective. If most boxes are ticked, revisit the list to prioritise

Figure 11.7 Desired Promotional Programmes

Example: 35mm camera market

Promotional Objectives (priorities)
- *Build high product awareness in TMS within 3 months*
- *Position product as 'the professional camera' against main challenger*
- *Generate sales leads for distribution chain*

Suggested Advertising and Promotions Programmes
including likely tools/techniques
- *Advertising campaign in the major amateur and professional trade press (including 0800 response)*
- *Point-of-sale material for dealers*
- *Press conference for trade press*
- *Lavish product brochure for 0800 response and dealers*
- *Run a competition with major amateur magazine*

Anticipated Budget Required

Advertising	*£500,000*
P-O-S	*£150,000*
Brochure	*£200,000*
0800	*£60,000*

Timing and Scheduling of Promotional Activity

Brief agency	*6 months before launch*
Book media	*2 months before launch*
Distribute P-O-S	*1 week before launch*
Press conference	*day of launch*
Ad campaign	*launch week + for 3 months*

Agency/Supplier
Super Ad Inc.

- Complete a form per targeted segment/market

1.3.3 Place: Marketing Channels

The *place* ingredient of the marketing mix concerns distribution issues: the activities that make products or services available to customers when and where they want to purchase them. Customers must be able to readily access the products they wish to purchase, but the business must aim to keep the total inventory, transport, communication, storage and materials handling costs as low as is possible.

A key decision for the business to make is the selection of an appropriate marketing channel. This must give due consideration to the nature of the target market and the product in question. The *marketing channel* is the route through which a product or service passes from manufacture to consumption. For example, JCB manufactures construction equipment but does not sell direct to its end-user customers; instead JCB has a network of independent dealerships. Kellogg's supplies some of the biggest supermarket groups directly, while also choosing to supply wholesalers and cash and carry operators which in turn supply smaller retailers and the catering industry. Kellogg's chooses not to deal directly with its householder customers. Farm shops, however, are examples of a supplier choosing to cut out the need for marketing channel intermediaries, dealing directly with consumers.

In the light of customer analyses, knowledge of key customer values (KCVs) and buying processes, and with an awareness of competitors' routes to market, the business must consider whether its existing selection of marketing channel (or channels) is appropriate. The adopted channel(s) must lead to satisfied customers, adequate profit margins and minimal bureaucracy. Related to this issue are concerns about power, conflict and control in the marketing channel. For example, the business should have an understanding of which players direct proceedings and dictate policies and initiatives. This is important because when selecting the players with which to deal in a marketing channel, sound working relationships which facilitate the business's desired aims and marketing strategies will be required. Inevitably this requires control mechanisms and 'policing' of selected channel players. For example, large supermarket chains such as Tesco and Sainsbury exert considerable power in their distribution channels. This is important if the businesses are to retain control of the merchandise which they stock.

Businesses must make deliberate decisions about physical distribution management issues. In most businesses these are handled by

Figure 11.8 Distribution Channel Structural Requirements

	Segment 1:	Segment 2:	Segment 3:	Segment 4:
Required Channel Structure	• • • • •	• • • • •	• • • • •	• • • • •
Principal Likely Players/ Possible Power Issues				
Level of Contact Required with Players to Smooth Relationships				
Actions Necessary to 'Police' Channel Players/ Control Their Activity				

- Describe the required marketing channel per target market segment and its likely members
- Discuss any anticipated power/control issues

specialist transport managers, but in a marketing context it is important to ensure that policies are likely to keep customers happy and be in line with identified KCVs and perhaps any related differential advantage. Similarly with stockholding policies: if availability and lead-times are fundamental to satisfying customers, inventory policies must facilitate required inventory holdings and allocations.

Figure 11.9 **Summary of Marketing Channel Policy Issues**

NB: This form only applies where dealers/distributors are involved in sales transactions
Example: UK truck market

Segment 1: _National Freight Companies_   **Requirement:** 24 hour support   Parts/maintenance support round the clock

Segment 2: _Owner Drivers_
         •   Regular contact min 6 p.a.
 Requirement: •   Weekend servicing available
         •   Parts delivery service

Segment 3: _____   **Requirement:**
Segment 4: _____   **Requirement:**
Overall Policy Changes:
Personnel and Service Improvements Required:
• State required dealer and distribution changes necessary to facilitate target market strategy and associated marketing programmes (a) per core segment, (b) overall in the territory

Place: action required

Place: on the charts provided summarise the required channel structures for each target market segment (Figure 11.8) and any changes now required to distribution policies (Figure 11.9). Figure 11.9 uses the UK truck market as an illustrative example. In cases where the business has only direct relationships with customers, these

Figure 11.10 *Sales Links Through Suppliers/Contractors*

NB: This form is only relevant to businesses which have direct relationships with customers

Market/Segment:

Nature of Links With Suppliers/Contractors/Consortium Partners

Scope for the Business to Use These Links for Sales Leads

Requirements to Enable the Business to Use These Links

- Existing links/working relationships with third parties or intermediaries such as suppliers, contractors, consortium partners may form the basis for generating sales leads if handled with such an aim
- Use this form to identify any such possibilities and actions required
- Note, this is more applicable to businesses with direct relationships with customers rather than through third party channel intermediaries

channel aspects are not going to be of great importance. However, there may be sales opportunities stemming from relationships with contractors or consultants and their contacts, plus from licensing (see Figure 11.10). Channels to market are important and links with suppliers can provide sales leads.

1.3.4 Price

Price commonly is defined as the value placed on what is exchanged between supplier and consumer: otherwise known as the amount a customer is prepared to pay for a good or service. Businesses which set prices lower than customers are prepared to pay may be ignoring revenue opportunities and may ultimately become financially unstable and vulnerable. Businesses which over-price their products risk alienating customers and giving competitors an edge. In such cases only the most brand loyal customers may continue to purchase the business's goods or services.

There are several factors which are known to affect pricing decisions:

- The competitive situation: companies must set prices which are consistent with the competitive situation operating in a particular market, in line with their competitive position and reflecting any recognised differential advantage which may facilitate higher prices.
- Prices must be consistent with company objectives. Businesses requiring a rapid increase in market share will have different price strategies (e.g. price reductions/cutting) than those requiring high profitability in the short term (when margins must be maintained).
- Price levels must not be set in isolation of other marketing mix variables. Each element must be consistent with the others so that a cohesive message is developed. A product with an 'up-market' positioning and image requires an appropriately 'high' price rather than a discount price, as well as a select channel of distribution and sales programme.
- Although in the short term businesses may set prices which deliberately do not cover their development, production, distribution and marketing costs – as they perhaps attempt to penetrate a market and establish market share – ultimately, long term survival depends on prices being set which cover costs and provide adequate profit margins.

- Companies must understand the importance which customers place on price, which will vary from target market to target market. All too often, businesses are reluctant to set higher price points when in fact customers may have sufficient need and positive brand attitude to be prepared to pay more than they are currently asked.
- In certain markets, national and local governments impose controls which impact on prices. In most countries and in the EU, consumer legislation exists to protect customers from unreasonable or unfair pricing.

Setting prices

Setting prices is frequently an area which marketing professionals regard with trepidation. Yet despite the confusion which may surround it, there is a straightforward sequential process for setting prices:

1. *Develop pricing objectives*: A variety of short and long term concerns will be important, including cash flow requirements, survival, profitability, return on investment, desired market share, the status quo of the market and product quality. For example, a paint manufacturer which is launching a new product may be most concerned about achieving rapid penetration and market share.

2. *Assess target market's ability to purchase and its evaluation of price*: Customers' sensitivity to price varies. It is essential to understand how price sensitive are target customers, their tolerance of high prices and their propensity to shop around. Customer tolerance will relate to income, economic conditions, brand positioning, competitors' offers and their perception of value. For example, sales of luxury items fall during periods of economic recession.

3. *Determine level of demand and analyse the relationship with cost and profit*: Many businesses find it useful to consider the likely purchase quantities at different price points. Technically this is referred to as the elasticity of demand – the effect of a small price change on the numbers of a product purchased. Price elasticity of demand equals per cent change in number demanded divided by per cent change in price. The point at which total costs (fixed and variable) are equal to the revenue generated is termed the *break-even point*. Calculating the break-even point at a number of different pricing levels allows a company to understand the relationship between costs and revenue and indicates the likely impact on the business of different pricing levels.

4. *Evaluate competitive pricing*: An understanding of how competitors set their prices and an awareness of their actual price points, helps a business determine the parameters within which its prices must be set. It must be considered, however, if the business has a differential advantage on which to build up its price levels over rivals.

5. *Choose a pricing policy*: Pricing policy is generally linked to corporate objectives and presents four broad approaches:

- Market Penetration Pricing: setting low prices relative to competitors in order to gain market share. Note, it is not always easy to subsequently raise prices to fully cover costs and profit requirements without alienating distributors and customers.
- Price Skimming: the use of very high prices in order to maximise profits in the short term. Only applicable for highly innovative, strongly desired products with negligible competition.
- Psychological Pricing: perceived value pricing based on what customers believe a product or service is worth, rather than rational analysis of cost structures and competitors' pricing.
- Promotional Pricing: special price levels – usually lower than normal – to increase sales in the short term, linked perhaps to sales promotions and the use of 'loss-leaders'.

6. *Select a pricing method*: This is the mechanical process through which price is set. The alternatives are as follows:

- Cost-driven pricing: cost-plus pricing, where prices are set at a level to allow a certain pre-determined percentage profit once all costs have been met.
- Competition-driven pricing: 'going-rate' pricing to reflect the prices set by competitors.
- Demand-driven pricing: variable pricing to reflect markets in which demand varies over time or seasons.

7. *Decide on a specific price*: At this stage, the business determines the actual price to set. This may be varied as the marketing mix is manipulated to reflect developments in the market place, consumers' behaviour and competitors' actions.

8. *Payment mechanisms*: Once a price is set, decisions must be made as to how rigid it is to remain. A list price could be negotiable, but to what extent? There may be discounts for bulk or regular orders. Credit terms and specialised payment terms may need to be offered in order to achieve desired pricing levels over time. The price

ingredient of the marketing mix is only partly made up of the setting of price levels. Processes and mechanisms must be in place which enable customers to pay easily for the business's goods and services.

Pricing: required action

For *Pricing*, state what pricing policy and price point changes are required. Owing to product or marketing mix differentiation, consider if there is an opportunity for premium pricing or increasing price levels. Thought should be given also to the closest competitor's pricing, as customers may well compare prices.

Some businesses are involved in bid pricing. In such cases it is helpful to be aware of what can be learned from competitors' bids. For example, what are customers' bid requirements? Why are bids lost? Any required fine-tuning or changes in the business's pricing/bidding policy and procedures for the target markets under review should then be detailed.

Figure 11.11 provides a summary of these key pricing issues. Commence by examining the overall required pricing policy. Then, segment by segment, determine required price levels for the business compared with existing achieved price levels and closest competitor's pricing. If there is a discrepancy between the current achieved price and the desired price, consider

a) why this discrepancy exists, and

b) what action is required to reduce the gap.

Note, the required action may well involve other elements of the marketing mix, particularly product modifications and promotional activity. When completing this form, care is needed to ensure that pricing is related to the identified desired brand positioning and to competitors' positionings.

Figure 11.11 **Summary of Pricing Policy and Pricing Levels**

Pricing Policy Requirements and Pricing Levels							
Summary of overall pricing policy requirements and - if applicable - bid policy							
Pricing	**The Business's Pricing**			**Principal Competitor's Pricing**		
Segment	Achieved Price (A)	Desired Price or Bid Price (D)	A-D (+/−) and Reason for Discrepancy	Product Name	Achieved Price (A)	Desired Price (D)	A-D (+/−)
1							
2							
3							
4							
5							
6							
7							
8							

Competitor's Name:

- Inevitably the analyses will have revealed the need to modify pricing. The stated strategy will also require changes to pricing policies. Explain the required pricing policy and pricing levels
- If there is a discrepancy between the current achieved pricing and desired pricing level, consider what remedial action is required
- If information is known about the leading competitor, include it. Identify the competitor
- If bid pricing is applicable and problems are known/realised, explain any required changes in the upper section of the form

11.3.5 People

Marketing exists to satisfy *people* – customers. People matter, too, within the business and its channel intermediaries. In order to implement marketing strategies and programmes, it is essential to have well trained and motivated staff, orientated to the recommended strategies and aims of the marketing plan. Personnel in the inter-mediaries in the marketing channel, such as dealerships and retailers, must be controlled to ensure the marketing plan is correctly im-plemented. All personnel dealing with customers must be able to provide the required levels of customer service, expertise, advice and guidance. The processes must be in place which simplify their task and facilitate customers' easy contact with employees.

People: action required

Figure 11.4 has already examined the participation of personnel in the context of the product offering. Figure 11.12 examines requirements in terms of the process of dealing with customers and customer liaison in order to implement the requirements of the marketing plan. If there are human resource issues raised by the implementation needs of the marketing plan – such as recruitment, training, motivation, reward, reporting and organisational structures – these should be detailed in Figure 11.13.

Figure 11.12 **Process/Customer Liaison Improvements Required**

Area Requiring Attention	Explanation/ Definition	Required Action
Market Information		
Product Information		
Flows of Information for Bids/Pricing		
Demonstrations		
Handling Enquiries		
Pre-Delivery Advice (e.g. Progress Meetings)		
Commercial Support to Customers		
Technical Support		
Back-up Advice		
Payment Conditions/ Consumer Credit		
Inter-Personnel Relationships		
Communication with Clients		
Handling Visits		
Communication with Suppliers		
Feedback to Clients/Suppliers		
Training		
Other:		
Other:		

- This is the business helping customers; making life easier for customers to deal with the business; improving flows of information and communications

Figure 11.13 **Human Resource Requirements**

Human Resource Requirements: Implementation of the Marketing Plan
Recruitment Needs: (purpose, type of personnel, scheduling)
Training Requirements: (aims, activity, scheduling, personnel)
Motivational Actions: (aims, targets, scheduling, personnel)
Reward Issues: (types, aims, reasons, priorities)
Reporting and Organisational Structural Changes: (nature of changes and rationale)
• Detail human resource concerns. Be specific

11.4 Summary

The core output from any marketing planning exercise must be detailed action plans which outline the marketing mix programmes for each target market. It is essential that these programmes aim to satisfy customers' needs and therefore relate to the identified key customer values (KCVs), taking account of market trends and the business's competitive position, while utilising fully any differential advantage held over rivals. The recommended marketing programmes must also endeavour to implement the desired brand positioning strategy in each target market.

This chapter has presented summary charts for all of the core elements of well constructed marketing programmes: product (or service) requirements, promotional activity, marketing channel selection and distribution control, pricing and payment issues, and personnel/customer service needs. Until *each* of these has been examined and *specific* recommendations made, the marketing planning process cannot be developed further and, ultimately, the determined marketing strategy will not be implemented.

12

Resources and Timing

12.1 Introduction

Many marketing plans produce detailed marketing mix action lists without following through to determining the full costs and whether all activities are viable, determining when the programmes need to run and whether there are any economies of scale for certain activities across product groups or market segments. All too often the tasks are not allocated to specific departments or managers, with the result that sensible and carefully considered recommendations are simply not implemented. This short chapter with three summary charts ensures that those involved in marketing planning cannot ignore the key considerations of budgets, timing and the allocation of responsibilities.

12.2 Scheduling, Resources and Responsibilities

The marketing mix recommendations will inevitably result in some changes in current activity and spending. Summarising the programme tasks will help show the extent of changes to existing programmes. In order to ensure effective implementation, it will be necessary to allocate responsibility to specific managers for specific tasks. In addition, clear guidelines for the timing (scheduling) of the programme tasks must be made so as to avoid clashes between product groups or across segments, to aid internal communications and to ensure the core marketing requirements take place. Managers must not be allowed to produce unrealistic and expensive 'wish lists'. This will require an appraisal of the costs of the recommended marketing activities, with an assessment of whether these are realistic.

Figure 12.1 presents a summary of these important issues, using the camera market as an illustrative example. Businesses which ignore these issues may find that no-one takes 'ownership' of the required actions and implementation will be jeopardised. For example, a Midlands-based specialist in industrial gears and bearings which offers service contracts to local businesses decided to extend its geographic coverage. Although the business modified its marketing programme accordingly, implementation was hindered because individuals within the business failed to take responsibility for dealing with the new area's customer enquiries.

Figure 12.1 **Summary of Programme Tasks, Timing and Costs**

Example: 35mm camera market

Programme Task	Person or Department Responsible	Date(s) for Activity	Anticipated Cost	Implications for the Business
Product Development	*R & D*	*Q1/Q2*	*£120,000*	
Wider Distribution	*Channel Sales*	*Q1/Q2*	*£40,000*	
Develop Launch Strategy	*Marketing/ Agency*	*Q2/Q3*	*£20,000*	
Research Clinics	*R & D/ Marketing*	*Q2/Q3*	*£20,000*	*May need to modify other products*
Launch Product	*Marketing Sales*	*Q5*	*£240,000*	*Will need to postpone development of NEEK*
		(Q = quarter)		

- The main marketing mix requirements from Chapter 11 should be entered in column 1.
- People must now take 'ownership' of identified actions from Chapter 11 and determine schedules and programme costs

It may be necessary to consolidate these details into summary statements of responsibilities by name/department, by month, and under convenient budget headings: see Figures 12.2 and 12.3, which use the camera market as an illustration. If external suppliers/agencies are contracted to deliver specific actions, for example in terms of promotional requirements, the appropriate details should be included.

Figure 12.2 **Summary of Responsibilities**

Example: 35mm camera market

Person or Department	Responsibility/ Task	Dates/ Timings	External Supplier/Agency
Marketing	Recruit panels for clinics from TMS	12 panel members per month April through Sept.	Supa-Research plc
R&D	Manufacture new product for clinics	Feb/March (20 products per month required)	
Marketing Agency (Supa-Research plc)	Book venue for clinics	March	Room-Book Ltd
Research Agency	Attend clinics. Report	April–Sept. October 17th	

- Allocate the tasks detailed in Figure 12.1 to individual managers or departments
- Specify when these activities must take place

Figure 12.3 **Summary of Costs and Budget Implications**

Example: 35mm camera market

Task	Cost	Budget Implications for the Business
Advertising campaign	*£150,000*	*Significant impact if awareness objectives not met*
Marketing research	*£20,000*	
Launch venues	*£60,000*	*Exceeds current budget limits*
Literature production	*£20,000*	*Minimal impact*

- Summarise the costs/budgets for each of the marketing programme activities detailed in Chapter 11
- Outline any implications from the combined totals of these costs

12.3 Summary

This brief chapter has brought to the marketing planning process an important set of considerations. For the plan to be actioned and the detailed marketing mix recommendations implemented, personnel must take on the responsibility of ensuring the recommended tasks take place, that clear schedules are produced and that full costings are determined with an assessment of the overall budgetary implications.

13

Additional Implications, On-going Needs and Monitoring the Marketing Plan's Effectiveness

13.1 Introduction

Inevitably, the detailed strategic and implementation recommendations made within the marketing plan will have implications for departments other than marketing. Product designers, production personnel, sales and distribution managers, personnel and treasury departments as well as senior management in the business will need to

a) understand the direction of the plan,

b) believe in its rationale and rigour of analysis,

c) agree to change some of their practices and activities, and

d) be fully briefed.

Achieving these objectives will almost certainly require some canvassing by the marketing planners.

No matter how much work goes into marketing planning, it is important to appreciate the transient nature of the analyses. Businesses will need, for example, to identify remaining information gaps, so that consideration can be given to specifying any required marketing research. The marketing mix requirements cannot all be actioned immediately: new product development takes time, customer service modifications require training and controls, distribution improvements may require lengthy negotiations and contractual changes with third parties. All of these issues must be highlighted so that appropriate action can be taken.

Finally, it is essential to consider how the marketing plan will be monitored. Will the planners know that the recommendations are being carried out? What attempts will be made to judge the effectiveness of the plan's recommendations? Against which benchmarks will such a judgement be made?

This chapter considers the implications of the marketing plan's recommendations for other departments within the business, the on-going work and research needs, plus the monitoring of the marketing plan's implementation and progress.

13.2 Wider Implications for the Business

The target market strategy recommendations and suggested support-ive marketing programmes will inevitably impact upon other func-tions within the business, particularly R&D, sales and perhaps on finance, partnerships, channels to market, facilities, production, and reliance on support from other sectors in the business. It is important to gauge the nature of these knock-on effects and their importance. Figure 13.1 offers a format for reviewing these issues and identifying who will be responsible for taking control of them. As before, the camera market is used to illustrate these points.

Figure 13.1 Summary of Anticipated Knock-on Impacts

Example: 35mm camera market

Area of Impact	Implication Required Action/By whom?
New Product meets sales targets in year one	*Finance to monitor*
New Product exceeds targets	*Manufacturing to plan for up to 10% increase in production in Q2 and 15% increase in Q3 and Q4*
New Product falls short of target	*Finance to monitor stock build-up and purchasing to cut schedules with suppliers in Q2 +*
	(Q = quarter year)

- Detail the likely knock-on impacts
- Consider the action required to facilitate the plan's unhindered implementation

13.3 On-going Needs

The analyses will have identified weaknesses in the business's marketing information. Consider the most pressing outstanding information needs and how best such marketing intelligence should be gathered. Figure 13.2 offers a format for recording these on-going needs. There will be aspects of the strategy and marketing mix requirements – such as internal structuring or operations, product ranges and customer service, marketing programmes and market development – which cannot be addressed immediately. As shown in Figure 13.3 for the truck market, these aspects of the plan's recommendations must still be considered.

Figure 13.2   On-going Marketing Research Requirements
Example: 35mm camera market

Information Gap	Likely Research Activity	Timing	Cost
Level of repeat purchases of FMCG	*In store research of purchasers, face to face focus groups of users*	*Q2* *Q3* *Q4*	*£60,000* *£60,000* *£80,000*
		(Q = quarter)	
• Specify required marketing research activity			

Figure 13.3 Medium-term Work Required Summary

Example: UK truck market

Area	Required Work
Internal Structuring/ Operations	*Combine Parts and Service function*
Market Development	*Expand market coverage in zones 1 and 3*
Resource Base	*Increase manufacturing capacity by 10% and 15% in next 2 years*
Products and Product Mix	*Phase out products with poor DPM positions. Launch one new product pa*
Sales Force and Customer Service	*Appoint Sales Director* *Increase sales force by 6 in zones 1 and 3*
Marketing Channels	*All Dealers to obtain ISO good for service support*
Promotional Activity/ Evaluation	*Maintain brand awareness vs competitor* *Increase activity in zones 1 and 3*
Pricing and Payment Terms	*Hold prices (cut costs). Extend payment terms from 30 to 60 days for Dealers who stock*
Training	*Improve customer care*
Recruitment	
Other:	

- Specify the longer-term marketing requirements

13.4 **Monitoring Effectiveness and Progress**

The final stage of any marketing planning exercise is to ensure that procedures are set up for monitoring the effectiveness of the plan. The importance of this aspect can readily be seen in any industry. For example, a builders' merchant which had suffered badly through the recession decided to undertake a leaflet drop advertising its product ranges and services. Although turnover increased slightly after the campaign, general trading conditions were also starting to improve, so it was difficult to appraise the success of the leaflet drop. There are two parts to this important monitoring stage of the process.

First, periodically review whether the stated marketing objectives (Chapter 10) have been achieved. Make a note of when the reviews will take place, what form they should follow and who will be involved. Formalising this part of the monitoring will help ensure that the review really happens. It is also important to check that the marketing planning process is improving the financial health and status of the business.

The second part of the monitoring process involves systematically updating the marketing analyses (Section II) as more information becomes available. Customer needs, competitors' strategies, market trends, SWOTs, bases for competing (DAs) and brand positionings will all be subject to change over time. By incorporating new information into the analyses, a useful impression is gained of the more subtle changes brought about by the marketing plan. The updating also gives a head start for developing the next period's plan, so a business which has carried out one planning cycle, should find the next very much easier.

It may be useful to complete Figure 13.4 to identify the business's performance in relation to the objectives set and other areas considered to be important. The monitored issues column has been left empty enabling a choice of which areas to revisit.

Figure 13.4 **Monitoring Performance Box**

Monitored Issue	Expected Result (6 mths)	Actual Outcome (6 mths)	Reason for Gap	Expected Result (12 mths)	Actual Outcome (12 mths)	Reason for Gap

- Determine measures for benchmarking progress
- Expected results should include sales, contributions, attitudinal data relating to customers' perceptions of brand positioning and their views on customer satisfaction

13.5 Summary

The marketing plan will have raised issues which affect other areas of the business outside the marketing function. These need to be considered and perhaps some canvassing of colleagues will be required to aid the unhindered implementation of the plan's recommendations. This chapter has considered these issues and provided forms for recording appropriate actions.

In addition, the chapter considers the marketing research and on-going marketing programme developments which cannot be immediately addressed but which – if the marketing plan is not to lose pace – must be tackled in the medium term. Finally, the marketing plan's implementation and effectiveness must be monitored against wide ranging and carefully thought out bench marks.

14

Managing a Marketing Planning Programme

14.1 Introduction: People and Cultures – Marketing Planning Must be Facilitated

Marketing planning is a process and should become a philosophy in marketing-orientated businesses. As detailed in this workbook, there are numerous stages and tasks. Perhaps before any groundwork is undertaken in initiating marketing planning, however, thought should be given to the nature of personnel to be involved in the marketing planning process, their concerns, abilities, chains of communication and command and level of motivation. The act of marketing planning itself must be managed and facilitated. Research has shown that without consideration of these issues, marketing planning will not be successful. This chapter's brief examination of these concerns should act as a warning. A checklist of 'people' and 'culture' considerations is presented by way of a conclusion. Consideration of these issues before marketing planning is instigated should help smooth the way for effective adoption of marketing planning and its requirements.

14.2 The Need for Guidance

Leading marketing strategist Nigel Piercy argues that 'the conventional route to putting together all the disparate bits and pieces [of marketing] – marketing strategies, marketing programmes, and marketing information – is via marketing planning'. He adds an important note of caution, however, stating that in practice if left to their own devices, most marketing managers do not make these links and will not. Without a formalised, well-structured and step-by-step procedure for marketing planning, Piercy's research has identified many instances where effective marketing planning has not occurred. Our own empirical work with numerous businesses in four Continents, indicates that Piercy is correct in his assertions, if managers are given no guidance. If assisted with a managed, controlled, formalised and on-going marketing planning programme – such as outlined in this workbook – managers will indeed pass through these essential stages of marketing analysis, strategy formulation and development of associated marketing programmes to facilitate their determined strategies. The result invariably is a well-structured, actionable marketing plan capable of benefiting the business significantly. In developing such a plan, participating managers will inevitably build improved relationships with immediate colleagues, managers in other functional areas, senior executives and with channel members.

14.3 Facilitating Implementation

Piercy focuses on the need to facilitate implementation, outlining the lack of attention devoted to the implementation in practice of both marketing strategies and marketing mix programmes. He believes – supported by numerous marketing experts – that inadequate attention is given to producing plans which address implementation. This is equally true in the published marketing literature and for experts putting together training and consultancy programmes. Piercy states that 'implementation *is* strategy', and that chief executives should 'reject out-of-hand any marketing plan of any kind which does not come with a detailed and realistic implementation strategy'. This is why the concluding chapters of this workbook concentrate on assigning responsibilities, budgets and time frames; in addressing the on-going work requirements, plus the importance of establishing benchmarking procedures to monitor progress and effectiveness.

14.4 Barriers to Implementation: People and Culture

Too much focus is given to techniques and formal methods in marketing strategy and management research. While grasping the tools and concepts is important, commitment and 'ownership' of marketing recommendations matter more. As Piercy explains, 'the rewards come from getting our marketing act together and getting people excited and motivated to do the things that matter to customers in the marketplace'. One of the fundamental weaknesses in most marketing initiatives is the failure to recognise the role of personnel and management practices and the neglect of incorporating associated actions into marketing implementation strategies. Corporate culture, management style, information flows, organisational structures and participation, 'are treated either as facilitating mechanisms or as mere context, to be set aside as trivial compared to the real business of complex analysis and plan-writing'. In fact, these organisational people issues are part of the process of marketing planning. How marketing planning is seen to be a process and how that process is in fact managed are crucial concerns which must be tackled specifically when determining implementation plans for marketing strategies and marketing programmes. The ethos of this workbook is that marketing planning is indeed a process and that if managed effectively, it is a process which brings innumerable benefits.

The conclusion by Nigel Piercy and planning expert Malcolm McDonald is that marketing planning must be managed. Piercy has concisely summed up the crucial issues to be considered, discussing three distinct planning dimensions. These must be addressed when instigating marketing planning initiatives and when considering how effective implementation of plans can be facilitated.

The Three Planning Dimensions:

1. *Analytical*: techniques, procedures, structure, iteration, written plan.

2. *Behavioural*: managerial perceptions, participation, strategic assumptions, motivation, commitment, 'ownership'.

3. *Organisational*: organisational structure, information, culture, management signals, mission and vision, norms and values.

Analytical dimension

To produce effective marketing plans, the correct tools for the job must be used and understood, to analyse problems and opportunities and identify the required solutions and strategies. This involves formal procedures and systems to organise planning, a structure to ensure planning is both comprehensive and manageable; iteration to facilitate debate and reflection of the dynamic nature of planning and markets; with a written plan to encapsulate conclusions and enable their communication. Training personnel in the required marketing skills is fundamentally important, but not sufficient alone to ensure effective implementation. Marketers must understand the essence of marketing planning, its aims and roles as outlined in the first section of this workbook. Participating managers must comprehend the required marketing analyses, the core strategic decisions and the complexities of the marketing programmes recommended, as detailed in this workbook. There is an additional requirement in marketing planning to consider behaviour and the organisation.

Behavioural dimension

Behavioural planning concerns how well planning and its activities are done, in addition to the worries about what actually is done. These issues have little connection with the tools and techniques of planning, but do affect what can be achieved in practice. For example, managers' preconceived views of marketing planning and their angsts; participation levels in planning and the attitudes of managers directly involved; any assumptions held by relevant line and senior managers about what they believe the business could and should achieve; the level of motivation to see that planning actually happens; commitment to make required changes and steer from the status quo; and, the ownership of the required marketing and organisational tasks to implement recommended marketing strategy and the detail of the marketing plan. These are clearly important issues and consideration must be given to these concerns prior to any marketing planning activity, during the planning work and particularly when ensuring implementation of the marketing plan takes place.

In particular, when finalising marketing recommendations and courses of action, it is important to consciously plan for recalcitrance, fear of uncertainty, political interests and planning avoidance or 'shirking'.

Organisational dimension

Most of these behavioural nuances are at least in part, if not totally, dictated by the context of the business itself. The organisational structure, flexibility, vested interests, capacity to get things done differ from company to company but must be considered in putting together marketing planning initiatives. Information is essential for effective planning, but what of the organisation's view of information, quantity, quality, availability, sharing, gatekeeping, confidentiality? All businesses have cultures. Some cultures are open and ready to adapt to new ways of tackling problems, while in other organisations there will need to be a more 'slowly, slowly' policy. It is worth watching for management signals which reveal managers' real attitudes to marketing planning and associated suggestions, along with hidden norms and values which will affect what managers can achieve or are prepared to attempt.

14.5 Overcoming Barriers Facing Effective Implementation

In addressing measures required to facilitate implementation of marketing plans, Malcolm McDonald emphasises the need to have committed personnel who are highly motivated, understand the underlying concepts of marketing, but who have good relationships with other functional areas and with all levels of the managerial hierarchy. Without an understanding of the people and organisational issues, marketing initiatives are not guaranteed to be successfully and effectively implemented. Nigel Piercy's views are perhaps stronger, arguing that these issues must be analysed and plans developed which deliberately address these internal organisational concerns if marketing plans and strategies are to be 'owned' by managers and put into practice with true conviction of purpose.

The first priority is to establish the concept of marketing planning and an understanding of the analysis, strategy, programmes for implementation process. Even in the early days of a marketing planning initiative, however, consideration should be given to the influences from company culture and personnel, the key personnel to include and the likely hurdles to be overcome. These issues will impact on the effectiveness of marketing planning and will need to be addressed. Implementation of marketing plans does not hinge purely on effective actioning of marketing mix recommendations. Internal people and organisational issues also play a part; during the planning process itself and when implementing marketing programmes.

The starting point has to be to identify personnel to be involved in any marketing planning initiative, the likely hurdles to be faced and the key associated actions.

There are six sets of managerial issues checklisted in Figure 14.1. Tackle each point's questions and consider, in the light of the responses, what actions will be required, by whom and when. Failure to address these concerns may limit the effectiveness of marketing planning.

Figure 14.1 Checklist of People and Cultural Concerns: Managing the Marketing Planning Process

People and Cultural Concerns: Managing The Marketing Planning Process	
1. Involvement	• Who should be involved in the marketing planning work and when? • Any additional personnel required intermittently? If so, who and when? • Who from senior management needs to be aware of the marketing planning exercise? • Who from senior management needs to participate in the marketing planning programme? • From which non-marketing areas could personnel usefully contribute to the marketing planning initiative (e.g. R&D, sales)?
2. Time Frames and Formats	• What is a realistic time frame for the marketing planning work? (For analysis, strategy formulation and development of programmes) • What is an appropriate format for the planning work? (work groups/individuals; by territory/ markets/ products; workshops/seminars/ conferences; documents/presentations; in work time/weekends) • What will be the required control and communication process for participating managers? (With senior manager responsible, between individuals and work groups)
3. Additional Resources	• Any immediately required resources to enable the marketing planning initiative itself to progress? (Manpower, telecoms, computing, data, budgets)
4. Participating Managers' Expectations	• What will be participating managers' expectations of marketing planning? • What will be participating managers' worries? • Will there be any cliques of managers to watch? • Will there be any petty 'office politics' to monitor?
5. Level of Command	• To facilitate the marketing planning initiation and to control the participating managers, what level of command and sense of direction will be required?
6. Additional Managerial and Operational Problems	• What other difficulties, managerial and operational, are likely to be encountered during the marketing planning initiative?
• Consideration of these people/cultural/operational issues - before marketing planning is instigated - should smooth the path for more effective acceptance of the marketing planning process and activities.	

14.6 Summary

Before marketing planning should be introduced to a business, senior management – particularly the marketing director – must consider the personnel who should be involved because of their line responsibilities, seniority or knowledge and experience. In all businesses there are inevitably cultural and personnel barriers facing the instigation of any formalised process, especially one which by its very nature will prove time consuming and taxing. The issues raised in this short chapter are fundamentally important. The consideration of whom to involve and when, lines of communication and senior management participation, has been proved to be an important aspect of marketing planning. In addition, decisions about time frames, extra resources required to conduct marketing planning tasks and ensuring those involved are positively motivated, are important concerns which should be addressed *prior* to the initiation of the marketing planning programme.

Section IV Checklist

By the end of this *Implementation* section of *The Marketing Planning Workbook* you should have:
- Produced detailed marketing mix programmes addressing:
  Products/services
  Promotion
  Place: marketing channels
  Pricing/payment
  Personnel/customer service
- Confirmed scheduling, resources and responsibilities for the recommended marketing programmes
- Considered additional implications, on-going work needs and the monitoring of the marketing plan's effectiveness
- Evaluated likely people and cultural barriers within the business facing successful marketing planning

Successful implementation of the determined marketing strategy requires comprehensive marketing mix programmes, clear allocation of schedules, budgets and responsibilities, the understanding of on-going requirements and a controlling assessment of the plan's progress.

The Marketing Planning Workbook

Section I
Perspective

Section II
Core Analyses

Section III
Analyses into Strategy

Section IV
Programmes for Implementation

Section V
The Marketing Plan Document

Section V

The Marketing Planning Document

With so much work complete, it is possible to become submerged with detailed documentation. This can mean that the core issues are in danger of becoming clouded and the principal thrusts of the marketing plan may be lost to the reader. The output of the marketing planning programme, the written plan, must be a concise yet well informed document, summarising key analyses, stating the determined marketing strategies, and presenting the detail of the implementation programmes. There are many possible formats for the marketing plan document. Section V reviews one popular structure which can be adopted.

- The marketing plan document
- Suggested plan contents

15

The Marketing Plan:
The Document

15.1 Introduction

The Marketing Planning Book has so far explained the rationale behind
marketing planning and presented a guide to the core steps of
marketing analysis, strategic thinking and development of marketing
programmes to facilitate implementation. The final task is to summarise these activities in a short report: the written marketing plan. There
are many formats for the plan, and many organisations have their own
bespoke template. This chapter outlines one popular running order.
The final document needs to be concise, yet complete in terms of
presenting a summary of the marketplace and the business's position,
explaining thoroughly the recommended strategy and containing the
detail of the required marketing mix actions.

15.2 A Suggested Blueprint

The marketing plan needs to be an informative, logical overview of the
work, ideas and recommendations so far produced: the analyses,
strategy recommendations and marketing programmes required for
implementation of the plan. Figure 15.1 presents a suggested running
order.

Figure 15.1 **Typical Marketing Plan Document Structure**

Section	Section Title	Typical No. Pages
1	Management or Executive Summary	2-3
2	Objectives Organisation's Mission Statement Detailed Organisation Objectives Product Group Goals	1
3	Product/Market Background Product Range Explanation Market Overview and Sales Summary	2-3*
4	SWOT Analysis Scene-Setting Overview	1-2*
5	Analysis Marketing Environment and Trends Customers Competitors	8-12*
6	Strategies Core Target Markets Basis for Competing/Differential Advantage Desired Brand/Product Positioning	3-5
7	Statement of Expected Results/Forecasts	1-2
8	Marketing Programmes Marketing Mixes Tasks and Responsibilities	8-12*
9	Financial Implications/Budgets	1-2
10	Operational Implications	1-2
11	Appendices SWOT details Information on competitors Background data and information Research findings in detail References	20+
•	* Likely to be supported with material in report appendices	

- *Management Summary* (or *Executive Summary*) should be a concise overview of the entire report, including key aims, overall strategies, fundamental conclusions and salient points regarding the suggested marketing programmes (marketing mixes). Few people will have sufficient time to read the entire report, tending to 'dip in' here and there, so the Management Summary must be both concise and informative.
- *Objectives* are for the benefit of the reader, to give perspective to the report. Aims, objectives and time frames should be stated briefly in this section.
- *Product/Market Background* is a necessary section: not everyone will be fully familiar with the products and their markets being discussed. This section 'scene-sets', aiding the reader's understanding of the marketing plan.
- The *SWOT* is an important foundation for any marketing plan, helping to produce realistic and meaningful recommendations. The section in the main body of the report should be kept to a concise overview, with detailed market by market or country by country SWOTs – and their full explanations – kept to the appendices of the report.
- The *Analysis* section is at the heart of the marketing planning exercise: if incomplete or over subjective, the recommendations are likely to be based on an inaccurate view of the market and the organisation's potential. This section gives a sound foundation to the recommendations and marketing programmes. It includes a summary of the analyses of market trends and the marketing environment, customers, competitor positions and competitors' strategies.
- *Strategies* should be self-evident if the analyses have been objective and thorough: which target markets are most beneficial to the organisation, what is to be the differential advantage or competitive edge in these markets, and what is the desired product positioning. This strategy statement must be realistic and detailed enough to action.
- Having highlighted the strategic thrust and intention, it is important to explain the *Expected Results* and sales volumes, to show why the suggested strategies should be followed.
- *Marketing Programme Recommendations* are the culmination of the various analyses and the statement of strategies: exactly what needs to be done, how and why. This section is the detailed presentation of the proposed marketing mix designed to achieve the goals and implement the strategies.

- The full picture may not be known, requiring input from other functional areas within the business outside marketing, but an indication of required resources and budgets, plus capital and revenue issues – the *Financial Implications* – must be given.
- These strategies and marketing programmes may have ramifications for other product groups and sectors, for R&D and engineering, etc. The *Operational Implications* must be indicated.

The report should be as concise as possible. The document must, though, tell the full story and include evidence and statistics which support the strategies and marketing programmes being recommended.

- The use of *Appendices* helps to keep the main body of the report concise and well focused. All appendices should be fully cross referenced within the report.

15.3 Summary

The written plan may well be all that certain key managers see of the marketing planning exercise – the weeks of analysis, debate and planning. The report must be short so as not to deter its reading, while comprehensive in presenting the core information from the background analyses, the strategy recommendations and their rationale, and the detail of the planned marketing actions. The story needs to be complete and the arguments tight. The recommendations and outlined actions clear and logical. The sense of direction for the business must be unambiguous.

Section V Checklist

By the end of this *The Marketing Planning Document* section of *The Marketing Planning Workbook* you should have:

- Reviewed a suggested blueprint of a comprehensive marketing plan

The Marketing Planning Workbook

Section I
Perspective

Section II
Core Analyses

Section III
Analyses into Strategy

Section IV
Programmes for Implementation

Section V
The Marketing Plan Document

Appendix A1

Forecasting

A1.1 Introduction

In marketing, forecasts of market size and market share are required to enable marketers to:

1. estimate market attractiveness,

2. monitor performance,

3. allocate resources effectively,

4. gear up production to meet demand:
   a) excess stocks cost money/use resources;
   b) too low production leads to missed sales/ customer and distributor unease.

All of these issues are integral to marketing planning and as explained in Chapters 10 and 15, sales forecasts are important elements of the final marketing plan. Most businesses produce sales forecasts, but for those without, this appendix presents a brief overview of the most popular techniques, with recommendations offered for further reading if required.

A1.2 Forecasting Models

This overview follows Naert and Leeflang's popular classification taken from *Building Implementable Marketing Models* (1978):

- Product Class Sales Model (or Industry Sales Model): total number of units of a product category purchased by the population of all spending units.
- Brand Sales Model: total number of units of a particular brand bought by the population of all spending units.
- Market Share Model: the relative number of units of a particular brand purchased by the total population; i.e. relative to the total number of units of the product class.

A1.3 Methods of Forecasting

Other than astrology and other methods of the occult, there are basically three categories of forecasting models for sales/marketing issues:

- Judgmental
- Time series and projection
- Causal

Each is now discussed in turn.

A1.4 Judgmental Sales Forecasting Models

A1.4.1 Sales Force Composite

This is simply where sales reps/field managers are asked to estimate their sales. The overall forecast is then arrived at by summing their forecasts.

- Widely used
- Relatively accurate over the short term (one or two quarters)
- Inexpensive
- Gives customer by customer record of expected sales/rep. in industrial markets. This is particularly useful for monitoring and evaluation of the sales force.

Problems:

- Difficult to motivate reps/field managers to take the time and be conscientious in forecasting
- Individual pessimistic/optimistic biases come to the fore
- Group/company biases are not ruled out. Therefore, must make allowances for biases.

The sales force/field managers tend to be highly aware of changes in likely customer purchases in the short term (the next few months), but often are unaware of broad economic trends or movements which are likely to affect customers' industries/clients. Therefore, this judgmental technique is weak in the longer term and in identifying turning points in underlying market trends.

A1.4.2 Expert Consensus

This is simply a jury of experts and opinions. Experts include marketers, marketing researchers, company executives, distributors, consultants, trade association officials, trade journal editors, and in some cases government agency officials. A very widely used technique.

There are basically three types: point forecasts, interval forecasts, probability distribution forecasts.

Point. Sales forecasts are for a specific amount of sales (i.e. an absolute amount with no room for mistakes or margin of error). Taken in isolation, particular point forecasts – for example a particular group of managers stating categorically that in one particular territory sales of a particular product will be 80,000 units over the next three months – can be prone to bias and error. It is, therefore, better to have several different points forecast by different groups of managers and to aggregate their predictions.

Interval forecasts. This is where a particular measure of confidence in the forecast is given. In other words, the above managers could be 80 per cent confident that 80,000 units will be sold in the three month period.

Probability forecasts. In this case, different forecasts for the same product in the same market are given with different percentage accuracies attached. For example, the above managers could be 80 per cent confident that sales of 80,000 units could be achieved, only 50 per cent confident that sales of 100,000 could be achieved, and only 10 per cent confident that 110,000 units could be achieved. This option allows the 'best' and 'most pessimistic' forecasts to be clearly identified.

The problem with using a jury of expert opinion is that there is a need to 'weight' the value of each expert's forecast. There are four methods for '*weighting*':

- Use equal weights (the simple averaging of all experts' forecasts, giving each expert equal prominence).
- Assign weights proportional to an assessment of each expert's level of expertise/knowledge/common sense.
- Assign weights proportional to a self-assessment of expertise (allow each expert to give a measure of his/her expertise).
- Use weights proportional to the relative accuracy of past forecasts

(i.e. look at how accurate each expert's forecast has been in the past and make allowances for the new forecasts accordingly).

There is no evidence that any one of these four methods of weighting is better than the others.

A1.4.3 Delphi

This is a commonly used approach and one recommended by many marketing researchers and consultants. The simple steps are:

1. Participants (e.g. field managers) make separate, individual forecasts

2. Central analyst (e.g. at HQ) independently aggregates these forecasts

3. A revised forecast is returned to each separate participant in the field

4. Participants then make revised forecasts in the context of the new 'picture'

5. The analyst at head office then centrally pulls the forecast together to produce the final overall forecast.

The Delphi technique avoids the weighting problems discussed above. The median of the group's overall response will tend to move towards a truer answer. This technique is useful for short-, medium-, and long-term forecasts, and also for new product developments where there is no historical information on which to base a forecast.

A1.5 Time Series Sales Forecasting Models

This is where a set of observations is evaluated to look for a trend. Generally by way of simple graphs, e.g. sales in units versus time. Typically then, sales per month or per quarter or per year over a particular period of time.

The assumption is that past patterns/changes can be used to predict the future.

It is important to identify the underlying trend, *ironed out* for cyclical, seasonal and random variation (statistical noise). Therefore, often averaged-out data are used.

A1.5.1 Naive

Characterised by a reliance on the last period's sales as a basis for forecasts for the next period's sales. Only useful if the underlying trend of sales is flat rather than at a particular peak or trough (in which case, a particularly good or bad period of sales would be used to forecast the next period's sales, even though the underlying trend may show that there is in reality no relationship between the two neighbouring periods). Typically for months or sales quarters.

A1.5.2 Moving Averages

This is where the average of the values for the last X periods is taken into account and updated – 'moved' – each period. In other words, were sales figures available for 8 periods, the newest sales figures would be added to make 9 periods in total. The average would be then taken for the most recent 8 periods, dropping the initial period (period number 1).

Typically, therefore, done for 8 periods ('the recent past').

> 'Sales for the next period would be equal to the average sales for the average of the last "X" [say 8] periods'

It would probably need adjusting by a number or seasonal index figure (e.g. c.–5 per cent for a known trough, or c.+8 per cent for a known high point in the seasonal pattern).

It is important to remember that this is a forecast suitable for predicting only 1 sales period in advance (1 month or 1 quarter). Its main use, therefore, is for inventory control for various standard items.

A1.5.3 Exponential Smoothing

This is a 'weighted' moving average. The more recent the period, the heavier the weight given; in other words the more recent the period the greater the importance re: the prediction. This assumes that more recent sales are a better indication of future sales. This work tends to be computer based, requiring complicated algorithms and statistical packages. There are various derivatives of this technique, such as Double Exponential Smoothing, Adaptive Smoothing, Winter's Extended Exponential Smoothing.

A1.5.4 Statistical Trend Analysis

This is the determination of the underlying trend or pattern of growth, stability or decline in a series of data. Typically based on simple regression analysis of Time vs. Sales. Orientated towards statistical computer packages, although some graphics packages can also undertake this task; e.g. Freelance.

A1.5.5 Box-Jenkins

Major economic cycles are inherent in sales patterns. With such cycles, most of the above techniques have been proved to be useless (they do not pick up the cycles). There is a need, therefore, for a Box-Jenkins routine: a specially designed statistical routine requiring computer support. The problem here is that there needs to be a minimum of 45 sales periods of information, but the routine does consider underlying cycles inherent in trends.

Note: clearly, there is a need to have managers' knowledge of expected market changes in any forecasting.

Before choosing a particular forecasting technique, it is important first to examine a plot of sales data and to visually eyeball the *pattern/trends* before deciding how far back in the data set to proceed and which technique to use.

Typically, it is better to use a combination of forecasting techniques and to aggregate the various forecasts to come up with one overall prediction of sales.

A1.6 Causal Sales Forecasting Models

Sales change over time due to changes in one or more market variables (e.g. competitor activity, price, etc.) other than simply time.

A1.6.1 Barometric

For example, marketers of baby food may argue that sales depend on levels of births (or do they?!). In construction, it could be that sales of backhoe diggers depend on the number of housing starts. Therefore it is important to attain data on sectors/industries relevant to a particular product's sales, and correlate this information with product sales. The problem is mainly one of false messages and of using several different indicators at once. Still, this is a useful technique for helping to explain some of the trends and patterns, or even helping to validate predictions resulting from some of the above time series or judgmental techniques.

A1.6.2 Buyer Intentions – Surveys

Surveys through marketing research of buyer intentions. If these surveys are undertaken at regular points in time, a plot can be made of the customer survey expectations of purchase intent against real sales occurring during similar periods. Over time, through graphs and simple correlation, the overall pattern can be identified and therefore the value/error of the predictions made from marketing research surveys can be quantified. These surveys can then be used on a regular basis knowing the expected margin of error to put on the claim for customer expectations of purchases. In other words, the evaluation of past surveys' results against real sales gives a weighting to future surveys' findings and their accuracy.

A1.6.3 Causal Regression

This is the most widely used causal model of forecasting. A multi-variable regression equation relates sales to various predictor variables such as disposable income, price relative to competitors, levels of advertising, numbers of products on the market, etc.

Multiple Regression Steps:

1. Identify (through discussions with management, previous research studies, etc) the relevant predictor (independent) variables.

2. Collect time series and cross-sectional data (time series data is the same information collected for various points in time; an historical record/trend. Cross-sectional data is a snapshot in time – in other words a one-off hit).

3. Identify whether the relationship between sales and predictor variables is linear (a straight line), or curvilinear (with various peaks and troughs).

4. Use regression on a standard computer package (e.g. *SPSS* or *Minitab*) to get the coefficients (each individual independent variable's weighting or relative impact) and percentage of accuracy. In other words, each of the predictor variables such as disposable income, price, etc. will have a different impact on sales and until all of

the relevant predictor/independent variables have been identified there will not be a high percentage level of accuracy for predictions (known as the R^2). In other words, if key market characteristics which determine sales are omitted, the level of accuracy will be low.

5. Repeat steps 1 to 4 adding in additional predictor variables until the overall R^2 – the level of predictive ability usually measured as a percentage – is good (over 70 per cent).

A1.6.4 Econometric Models

Mathematical analogues and equations using multivariate statistical techniques similar to regression but more complicated. (AID, factor analysis, etc.).

A1.7 Sales Forecasting: Summary

Overall, it is widely believed that the causal techniques are better than judgmental. However, time, data and resources are not always available for causal modelling.

Within the judgmental category, no one technique has been proved to be better than the others, although the *Delphi* technique is extremely popular and widely used.

Within the causal approach, it is again hard to prove that one technique is better than others. The barometric approach and buyer intention survey are both widely used and can be extremely useful in explaining/describing forecasts made using the more statistical techniques or time series graphs. Of the statistical techniques, *causal regression* (taking into account many marketing variables) has been shown to be a very useful technique.

The overall conclusion is that it is better to use a mixture of forecasting techniques rather than just one. The *Delphi* technique is an extremely useful one to consider, supported in the first place by simple *time series graphs* and the moving averages approach. In order to explain some of these trends, it is useful then to look at the *barometric* approach (specifically looking at how sales of products compare with customers' sales; e.g. housing starts if supplying construction equipment). Often in the slightly longer term, owing to resources, it is a beneficial exercise to develop a simple *multiple regression* model which once developed, will run on a very straightforward spreadsheet package, such as *Lotus 123*.

A1.8 *Useful References*

See the following references in the Bibliography: Harvard Business Review (1991), Lilien and Kotler (1983), Naert and Leeflang (1978), Tull and Hawkins (1990).

Appendix A2

Blank Master Proformas

Note: These are available from the publisher on disk.

- Summary of Existing Target Market Segments (2.1)
- Importance of Current Markets (2.2)
- The ABC Sales: Contribution Chart (2.4)

- Core Market Trends and Predictions (3.1)
- The Marketing Environment Issues (3.2)

- The SWOT Analysis In Planning (4.2)

- Customers, KCVs, Buying Process Steps and Core Influences (5.3)

- Competitive Positions and Differential Advantage (6.2)

- Information Required for the DPM Analysis (7.4)
- The DPM (7.5)
- The Stages of the PLC (7.7)

- Mission Statement Summary (8.1)
- Determination of Target Markets (8.3)

- Identification of DAs (9.1)
- The Positioning Map (9.3)
- Target Marketing Strategy Summary Statement (9.4)

- Marketing Objectives (10.1)
- The Gap Chart (10.2)
- Corrective Actions Required to Close the Gap (10.3)

- Summary by Segment of KCVs and DAs (11.1)
- Customer Perceptions: the Need for Change (11.2)
- Summary of Required Product/Service Mix (11.3)
- Required Service Levels to Support Product Mix (11.4)
- Summary of Current Advertising and Promotion (11.5)
- Key Promotional Activity Required (11.6)
- Desired Promotional Programmes (11.7)
- Distribution Channel Structural Requirements (11.8)
- Summary of Marketing Channel Structural Requirements (11.9)
- Sales Links Through Suppliers/Contractors (11.10)

- Summary of Pricing Policy and Pricing Levels (11.11)
- Process/Customer Liaison Improvements Required (11.12)
- Human Resource Requirements (11.13)

- Summary of Programme Tasks, Timing and Costs (12.1)
- Summary of Responsibilities (12.2)
- Summary of Costs and Budget Implications (12.3)

- Summary of Anticipated Knock-on Impacts (13.1)
- On-going Marketing Research Requirements (13.2)
- Medium-Term Work Required Summary (13.3)
- Monitoring Performance Box (13.4)

Figure 2.1 **Summary of Existing Target Market Segments**

Customer Group or Market Segment	These Customers' Key Needs (KCVs)	Adopted Descriptions Used by the Business to Describe Target Market Segment
1		
2		
3		
4		
5		
6		

- Rank segments in column 1 in order of importance to the business
- For each segment, rank the KCVs listed in column 2
- Define KCV term if required so as to avoid ambiguity

Figure 2.2 **Importance of Current Markets, Last 10 Years**

Rank Order of Markets by Year (Current year = t)										
Segment	t-9	t-8	t-7	t-6	t-5	t-4	t-3	t-2	t-1	t
1										
2										
3										
4										
5										
6										
7										
8										

Reasons for Major Changes

- Rank each market's importance over the years. Importance may be in terms of sales volumes, market share, profitability or contribution
- Explain any major changes in rank position year on year

Figure 2.4 **The ABC Sales: Contribution Chart**

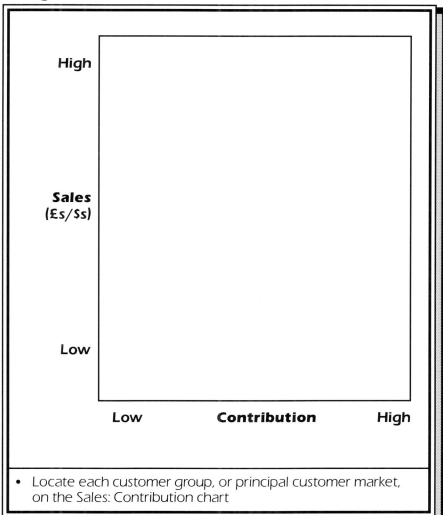

High

Sales
(£s/$s)

Low

Low   **Contribution**   High

• Locate each customer group, or principal customer market, on the Sales: Contribution chart

Figure 3.1 Core Market Trends and Predictions

Year	Sales Volumes (Units)	Sales (£s/$s) 000's	Profitabilty (£s/$s) 000's	Market Size	Business's Market Share	Number of Customers	Number of Main Competi-tors
t-5							
t-4							
t-3							
t-2							
t-1							
current year (t)							
t+1							
t+2							
t+3							
t+4							
Market:							

- Complete as many columns as possible
- Information beyond the current year is based on predictions
- For many markets, the business will not know market shares
- Principal customers: most businesses have an '80:20' split - the bulk of sales (e.g. '80%') comes from a minority of customers (e.g. '20%')
- Principal competitors (direct) indicate the level of market activity and, to a degree, the 'attractiveness' of the market

Figure 3.2 **The Marketing Environment Issues**

Summary of Core Issues

Macro Environment
(legal, regulatory and political, societal, technological, economic)

Micro Environment
(direct and substitute competition, new entrants, supplier influence, customer buying power)

Principal Implications to the Business of These Issues

- Consider the wide range of potentially relevant aspects
- Be prudent and objective - list only important concerns
- List the most pressing/crucial issues first
- Have evidence to support these assertions
- Have facts with sources with which to defend statements

Figure 4.2 **The SWOT Analysis in Planning**

Strengths	Weaknesses
Opportunities	**Threats**

- Rank (list) points in order of importance
- Only include key points/issues
- Have evidence to support these points
- Strengths and Weaknesses should be relative to main competitors
- Strengths and Weaknesses are *internal* issues
- Opportunities and Threats are *external* competitive and marketing environment issues

What are the core implications from these issues?

Figure 5.3   *Customers, KCVs, Buying Process Steps and Core Influences*

For each segment fill in the following details:

Customer Profile   Buying Process   Influences

KCVs

- Record the buying process, influences on each stage, typical customer profile and KCVs for each customer group or market segment.
- Number the *Influences* and indicate on the arrows which *Influences* apply to each step in the *Buying Process*.

Figure 6.2 Competitive Positions and Differential Advantage

Competitive Position	Segment:	Segment:	Segment:
Market Leader: • **Market Share Change** • **KCVs Offered** • **DA (if any)**	- - - - -	- - - - -	- - - - -
Challenger 1: • **Market Share Change** • **KCVs Offered** • **DA (if any)**	- - - - -	- - - - -	- - - - -
Challenger 2: • **Market Share Change** • **KCVs Offered** • **DA (if any)**	- - - - -	- - - - -	- - - - -
Challenger 3: • **Market Share Change** • **KCVs Offered** • **DA (if any)**	- - - - -	- - - - -	- - - - -
Fast Mover: • **Market Share Change** • **KCVs Offered** • **DA (if any)**	- - - - -	- - - - -	- - - - -
Follower: • **Market Share Change** • **KCVs Offered** • **DA (if any)**	- - - - -	- - - - -	- - - - -
Nicher: • **Market Share change** • **KCVs Offered** • **DA (if any)**	- - - - -	- - - - -	- - - - -

- Record the competitive positions for each segment
- The KCVs on this chart are those KCVs that each competitor is able to match
- Most companies do not have a DA (differential advantage), so this slot may be left blank for many companies
- There is *no* need to list actual %s for market share changes, current year versus last year. Key to market share entries: ++ large market share increase; + small market share increase; – small market share decline; –– large market share decline

Figure 7.4 **Information Required for the DPM Analysis**

Market Attractiveness

Factors	Score	Weighting	Ranking

Business/Competitive Position

Factors	Score	Weighting	Ranking

- Select the factors felt to be most important. Complete the columns
- This information now needs to be plotted on a graph, 7.5, as in Figure 7.2

What are the Implications from this Analysis?

Figure 7.5 **The DPM**

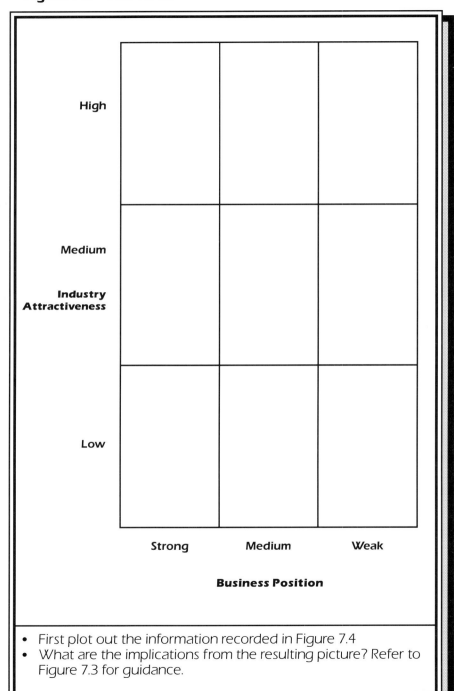

- First plot out the information recorded in Figure 7.4
- What are the implications from the resulting picture? Refer to Figure 7.3 for guidance.

Figure 7.7 **The Stages of the PLC**

Segment and Product	PLC Stage	Implications

- For each product in each segment indicate the stage in the PLC reached – in column 2
- In column 3, suggest the more obvious strategic implications for each product

Figure 8.1 **Mission Statement Summary**

Summary of the Business's Mission or Purpose
Corporate Mission Statement for the Business:
Mission Statement Relating to the Marketing Function:
• Use Figure 8.1 to (a) summarise the overall stated corporate mission – or sense of purpose – for the business, and (b) put this into a marketing context in terms of required marketing objectives

Figure 8.3 **Determination of Target Markets**

Market Segment Name (list in order of priority)	Characteristics of Market	Criteria: Reasons for Selecting as a Target Priority?	Existing Product/Service Offered

- List target markets in order of importance (rank)
- State why each market is important
- Summarise the products offered to each market

Figure 9.1 **Identification of DAs**

Segment Name	Identified Advantages (Strengths) for the Business Over Rivals	Are Advantages Sufficient Basis for a DA (Differential Advantage)?
1		
2		
3		
4		
5		
6		
7		
8		

- Record any DAs held by the business over rivals
- Remember a strength is only a possible DA if target customers desire it and rivals do not offer it
- To qualify as a DA, the strength must be cost effective and in the short term, defensible

Figure 9.3 **The Positioning Map**

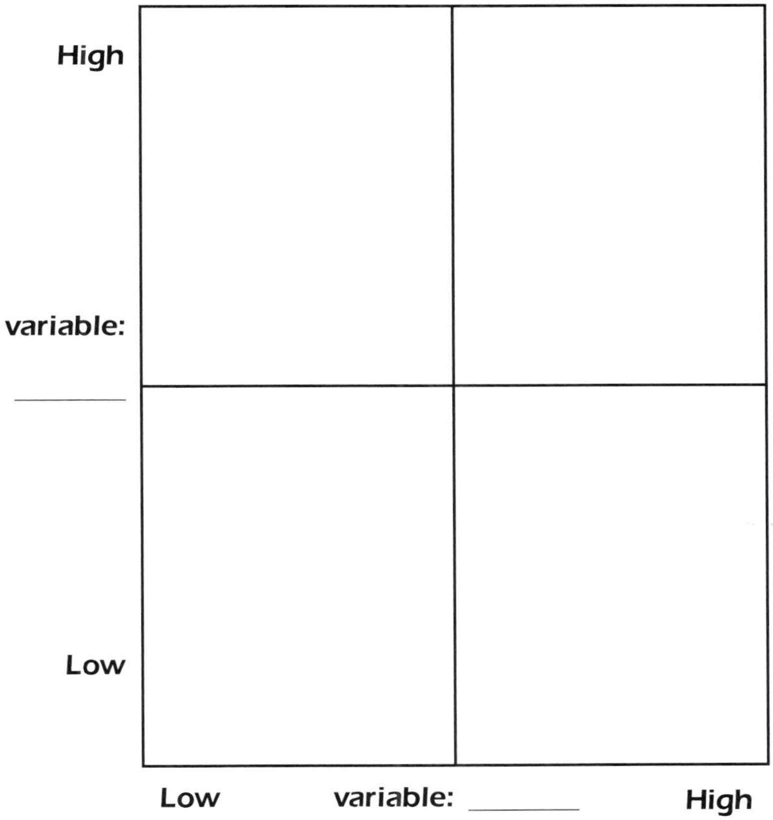

High

variable:
_____

Low

Low   variable: _____   High

- Let customer feedback specify the KCVs to use on the map's axes
- Plot customers' perceptions of the relative positionings (locations) on the map of the business's and leading competitors' brands or products

Figure 9.4 Target Marketing Strategy Summary Statement

Core Targeted Segments/Markets						
Segment	1:	2:	3:	4:	5:	6:
Principal Reason for Segment Being Target Priority						
Likely Sales Current Year (units) Likely Sales Next Year						
KCVs per Segment						
Required Brand Positioning						
Main Two Competitors						
Principal Competitive Threat						
Differential Advantage (DA)						
Key Problems to Overcome						
Capital Implications from Strategy						
• This is the overall statement of target market strategy and must be fully completed						

Figure 10.1 **Marketing Objectives**

General Strategic Marketing Objectives	
•	
•	
•	
•	
•	
•	
Segment:	**Objective:**
Segment:	**Objective:**
Segment:	**Objective:**
Segment:	**Objective:**
Segment:	**Objective:**
Segment:	**Objective:**

- First list overall marketing objectives
- Indicate the most important differences for key segments
- Include a time scale for each objective

Figure 10.2 **The Gap Chart**

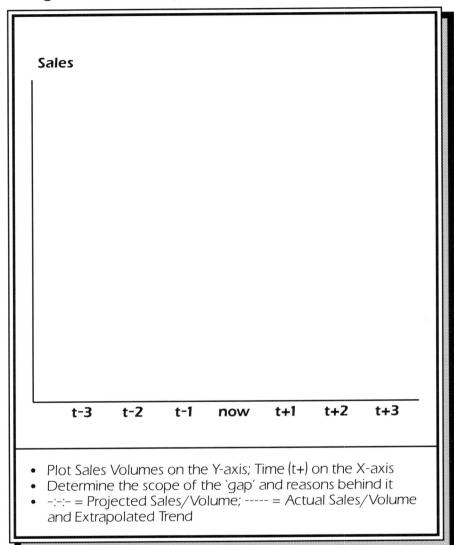

- Plot Sales Volumes on the Y-axis; Time (t+) on the X-axis
- Determine the scope of the 'gap' and reasons behind it
- -:-:- = Projected Sales/Volume; ----- = Actual Sales/Volume and Extrapolated Trend

Figure 10.3 Corrective Actions Required to Close the Gap

Corrective Action 1: Productivity	
Better product mix	Description?
More sales calls	Such as? To whom?
Better sales calls	In what manner?
Cost reduction	How?
Increase price	To what? With what implications?
Reduced discounts	Of what? To whom? When?
Improved asset utilisation	Such as?
Other: _____	
Other: _____	

Figure 10.3 (continued)

Corrective Action 2: Ansoff's Strategic Options

PRODUCT

	Present	New
Present	**Market Penetration Possibilities:** • • • •	**Product Development Requirements:** • • • •
New	**Market Development Opportunities:** • • • •	**Diversification:** • • • •

MARKET

- Consider the options available in closing the gap
- State what corrective action is now required or possible
- Be as detailed/specific as possible
- Be realistic: do not present over-extensive lists

Figure 11.1 **Summary by Segment of KCVs and DAs**

	Segment 1:	Segment 2:	Segment 3:	Segment 4:	Segment 5:	Segment 6:
Summary of KCVs						
Main Competitive Threat to the Company						
Any company DA? What?						
Desired positioning						

Figure 11.2 Customer Perceptions: the Need for Change – The Business vs Leading Rivals

	Current Perceptions:				
	Positive		Neutral	Negative	
	++	+	+/−	−	− −
Brand Awareness					
Product Awareness					
Product/Brand Image					
Quality of Product/ Deliverable					
After Sales Liaison/Support					
Value of Product/ Deliverable					
Product Performance					
On-Time Delivery					
Service Professionalism					
Technical Expertise					
Other:					
Other:					
Other:					

NB: Competitor 1 is: **Competitor 2 is:**

- Produce one form per targeted segment
- First enter the business's rating: ++, +, +/−, − or − −. NB: ++ = very positive/good; +/− = neutral; − − = highly negative/very poor
- Second enter the ratings for the two leading rivals in the segment
- Use this coding to mark companies on the chart: B = the business; 1 = main rival; 2 = second main rival. Name these competitors on the figure

In the context of these perceptions and standing versus leading rivals, on which features must the business work immediately?

Figure 11.3 **Summary of Required Product/Service Mix**

Segment/ Market	Title of the Business's Relevant Product or Service	Product or Service Description
1		
2		
3		
4		

- List out existing products/services pertinent to each target segment's needs and KCVs
- Column 2 = popular name/acronym within the business; column 3 = the common usage description meaningful to the customers

Segment/ Market	Additional Product/Service Requirements	Product/Service Attributes	Rationale

- In this section, detail any new/additional products needed in the light of the marketing analyses to maintain the business's competitive position or facilitate the business's target market strategy
- Note, the 'new product' could be a hybrid of activities which cuts across the business's divisions/departments/sectors

Figure 11.4 Required Service Levels to Support Product Mix

	Segment 1:	Segment 2:	Segment 3:	Segment 4:
People				
Advice/ Guidance (not consultancy)				
On-Going Support				
Facilities				
Other:				
Other:				
Any Training Requirements?				
Resource Implications				

- This table requests information concerning service aspects of the product offer. The products *per se* (their tangible attributes) are detailed in Figure 11.3
- Some service aspects will require retraining/orientation of personnel interfacing with customers
- These 'soft' issues connected with the product offering – such as warranties, technical advice, consumer finance, parts availability, etc.- inevitably will require resourcing

Figure 11.5 Summary of Current Advertising and Promotion

Nature of Campaign
What was done, when, which promotional mix elements

Campaign Objectives
For example, create brand awareness; generate sales leads; counteract rival's campaign; support new product launch; etc.

Cost of Programme (if known)

Results of Programme (if known)

- Complete a form per targeted segment
- Note: the promotional mix includes advertising, publicity and public relations, sales promotion, personal selling, sponsorship, direct mail and literature - all forms of promotional activity

Figure 11.6 **Key Promotional Activity Required**

Promotional Task	Targeted Segments							
	1	2	3	4	5	6	7	8
Build brand awareness								
Build brand image								
Build product awareness								
Build product image								
Position against competitors								
Re-position against competitors								
Create primary demand for product								
Influence customers' KCVs								
Generate sales leads								
Promote after-sales support								
Promote dealers/ distributors								
Support dealers' promotions								
Promote customer credit								
Influence customer buying process								
Other:								
Other:								

- Indicate promotional requirements per targeted segment
- Keep selections to the bare minimum - too many will not be feasible or cost effective. If most boxes are ticked, revisit the list to prioritise

Figure 11.7 **Desired Promotional Programmes**

Promotional Objectives (priorities)
Suggested Advertising and Promotions Programmes including likely tools/techniques
Anticipated Budget Required
Timing and Scheduling of Promotional Activity
Agency/Supplier
• Complete a form per targeted segment/market

Figure 11.8 **Distribution Channel Structural Requirements**

	Segment 1:	Segment 2:	Segment 3:	Segment 4:
Required Channel Structure	• • • • •	• • • • •	• • • • •	• • • • •
Principal Likely Players/ Possible Power Issues				
Level of Contact Required with Players to Smooth Relationships				
Actions Necessary to 'Police' Channel Players/ Control Their Activity				

- Describe the required marketing channel per target market segment and its likely members
- Discuss any anticipated power/control issues

Figure 11.9 **Summary of Marketing Channel Policy Issues**

NB: This form only applies where dealers/distributors are involved in sales transactions

Segment 1: _____   **Requirement:**
Segment 2: _____   **Requirement:**
Segment 3: _____   **Requirement:**
Segment 4: _____   **Requirement:**
Overall Policy Changes:
Personnel and Service Improvements Required:
• State required dealer and distribution changes necessary to facilitate target market strategy and associated marketing programmes (a) per core segment, (b) overall in the territory

Figure 11.10   *Sales Links Through Suppliers/Contractors*
NB: This form is only relevant to businesses which have direct relationships with customers

Market/Segment:
Nature of Links With Suppliers/Contractors/Consortium Partners
Scope for the Business to Use These Links for Sales Leads
Requirements to Enable the Business to Use These Links
• Existing links/working relationships with third parties or intermediaries such as suppliers, contractors, consortium partners may form the basis for generating sales leads if handled with such an aim   • Use this form to identify any such possibilities and actions required   • Note, this is more applicable to businesses with direct relationships with customers rather than through third party channel intermediaries

Figure 11.11 **Summary of Pricing Policy and Pricing Levels**

Pricing Policy Requirements and Pricing Levels							
Summary of overall pricing policy requirements and - if applicable - bid policy							
Pricing	**The Business's Pricing**			**Principal Competitor's Pricing**			
Segment	Achieved Price (A)	Desired Price or Bid Price (D)	A-D (+/−) and Reason for Discrepancy	Product Name	Achieved Price (A)	Desired Price (D)	A-D (+/−)
1							
2							
3							
4							
5							
6							
7							
8							

Competitor's Name:

- Inevitably the analyses will have revealed the need to modify pricing. The stated strategy will also require changes to pricing policies. Explain the required pricing policy and pricing levels
- If there is a discrepancy between the current achieved pricing and desired pricing level, consider what remedial action is required
- If information is known about the leading competitor, include it. Identify the competitor
- If bid pricing is applicable and problems are known/realised, explain any required changes in the upper section of the form

Figure 11.12 **Process/Customer Liaison Improvements Required**

Area Requiring Attention	Explanation/ Definition	Required Action
Market Information		
Product Information		
Flows of Information for Bids/Pricing		
Demonstrations		
Handling Enquiries		
Pre-Delivery Advice (e.g. Progress Meetings)		
Commercial Support to Customers		
Technical Support		
Back-up Advice		
Payment Conditions/ Consumer Credit		
Inter-Personnel Relationships		
Communication with Clients		
Handling Visits		
Communication with Suppliers		
Feedback to Clients/Suppliers		
Training		
Other:		
Other:		

* This is the business helping customers; making life easier for customers to deal with the business; improving flows of information and communications

Figure 11.13 **Human Resource Requirements**

Human Resource Requirements: Implementation of the Marketing Plan
Recruitment Needs: (purpose, type of personnel, scheduling)
Training Requirements: (aims, activity, scheduling, personnel)
Motivational Actions: (aims, targets, scheduling, personnel)
Reward Issues: (types, aims, reasons, priorities)
Reporting and Organisational Structural Changes: (nature of changes and rationale)
▪ Detail human resource concerns. Be specific

Figure 12.1 *Summary of Programme Tasks, Timing and Costs*

Programme Task	Person or Department Responsible	Date(s) for Activity	Anticipated Cost	Implications for the Business

- The main marketing mix requirements from Chapter 11 should be entered in column 1.
- People must now take 'ownership' of identified actions from Chapter 11 and determine schedules and programme costs

Figure 12.2 **Summary of Responsibilities**

Person or Department	Responsibility/ Task	Dates/ Timings	External Supplier/Agency

- Allocate the tasks detailed in Figure 12.1 to individual managers or departments
- Specify when these activities must take place

Figure 12.3 **Summary of Costs and Budget Implications**

Task	Cost	Budget Implications for the Business

- Summarise the costs/budgets for each of the marketing programme activities detailed in Chapter 11
- Outline any implications from the combined totals of these costs

Figure 13.1 **Summary of Anticipated Knock-on Impacts**

Area of Impact	Implication Required Action/By whom?

- Detail the likely knock-on impacts
- Consider the action required to facilitate the plan's unhindered implementation

Figure 13.2 **On-going Marketing Research Requirements**

Information Gap	Likely Research Activity	Timing	Cost

- Specify required marketing research activity

Figure 13.3 **Medium-term Work Required Summary**

Area	Required Work
Internal Structuring/ Operations	
Market Development	
Resource Base	
Products and Product Mix	
Sales Force and Customer Service	
Marketing Channels	
Promotional Activity/ Evaluation	
Pricing and Payment Terms	
Training	
Recruitment	
Other:	

• Specify the longer-term marketing requirements

Figure 13.4 **Monitoring Performance Box**

Monitored Issue	Expected Result (6 mths)	Actual Outcome (6 mths)	Reason for Gap	Expected Result (12 mths)	Actual Outcome (12 mths)	Reason for Gap

- Determine measures for benchmarking progress
- Expected results should include sales, contributions, attitudinal data relating to customers' perceptions of brand positioning and their views on customer satisfaction

Bibliography

Aaker, D.A. and Shansby, J.G. (1982) 'Positioning Your Product', *Business Horizons*, May–June, pp. 56–62.

Assael, H. (1992) *Consumer Behavior and Marketing Action*, Boston: PWS-Kent.

Bonoma, T.V. (1985) *The Marketing Edge: Making Strategy Work*, New York: Free Press.

Crowner, R.P. (1991) *Developing a Strategic Business Plan With Cases: An Entrepreneur's Advantage*, Homewood, Illinois: Irwin.

Day, G.S. (1984) *Strategic Market Planning: The Pursuit of Competitive Advantage*, St Paul, MN: West.

Dibb, S. and Simkin, L. (1991) 'Targeting, Segments and Positioning', *International Journal of Retail and Distribution Management*, 19 (3), pp. 4–10.

—— (1994) *The Marketing Casebook*, London: Routledge.

Dibb, S., Simkin, L., Pride, W. and Ferrell, O.C. (1994) *Marketing: Concepts and Strategies*, Boston: Houghton Mifflin.

Dickson, P.R. (1994) *Marketing Management*, Fort Worth: Dryden.

Doyle, P., Saunders, J. and Wong, V. (1986) 'A Comparative Study of Japanese Marketing Strategies in the British Market', *Journal of International Business Studies*, 17 (1).

Ford, D. (1990) *Understanding Business Markets*, London: Academic Press.

Giles, W. (1989) 'Marketing Planning for Maximum Growth', *Marketing Intelligence and Planning*, 3 (7), pp. 1–98.

Greenley, G. (1986) 'An Overview of Marketing Planning in UK Manufacturing Companies', *European Journal of Marketing*, 16 (7), pp. 3–15.

Harvard Business Review (1991) *Accurate Business Forecasting*, Boston: Harvard Business Review Paperbacks.

Hax, A.C. and Majluf, N.S. (1990) 'The Use of the Industry Attractiveness-Business Strength Matrix in Strategic Planning', in R. Dyson (ed.), *Strategic Planning: Models and Analytical Techniques*, Chichester: J. Wiley, pp. 73–92.

Hedley, B. (1977) 'Strategy and the "Business Portfolio"', *Long Range Planning*, 10, February, pp. 9–15.

Hooley, G.J. and Saunders, J. (1993) *Competitive Positioning, the Key to Market Success*, New York, London: Prentice-Hall.

Hutt, M.D. and Speh, T.W. (1992) *Business Marketing Management: A Strategic View of Industrial and Organizational Markets*, Fort Worth: The Dryden Press.

Jain, S. (1993) *Marketing Planning and Strategy*, Cincinnati: South Western Publishing Company.

Kotler, P. (1994) *Marketing Management: Analysis, Planning, Implementation and Control*, Hemel Hempstead: Prentice-Hall.

Lancaster, G. (1994) 'Planning a Campaign', in N. Hart (ed.) *Effective Industrial Marketing*, London: Kogan Page.

Lehmann, D.R. and Winner, R.S. (1988) *Analysis for Marketing Planning*, Plano: Business Publications.

Lilien, G.L. and Kotler, P. (1983) *Marketing Decision Making*, New York: Harper & Row.

Lockyer, K. (1983) *Production Management*, London: Pitman.

McDonald, M. (1982) 'International Marketing Planning', *European Journal of Marketing*, 16 (2), pp. 3–32.

———— (1992a) 'Ten Barriers to Marketing Planning', *Journal of Business and Industrial Marketing*, 7 (1), pp. 5–18.

———— (1992b) 'Strategic Marketing Planning: a State-of-the-Art Review', *Marketing Intelligence and Planning*, 10 (4), pp. 4–22.

McDonald, M. (1995) *Marketing Plans*, Oxford: Butterworth-Heinemann.

McDonald, M. and Leppard, J. (1993) *The Marketing Audit*, Oxford: Butterworth-Heinemann.

Naert, P. and Leeflang, P. (1978) *Building Implementable Marketing Models*, Leiden: Martinus Nijhoff.

Pearson, G. and Proctor, T. (1994) 'The Modern Framework for Marketing Planning', *Marketing Intelligence and Planning*, 12 (4), pp. 22–6.

Piercy, N. (1989) 'Diagnosing and Solving Implementation Problems in Strategic Planning', *Journal of General Management*, 15 (1), pp. 19–38.

———— (1990) 'Marketing Concepts and Action: Implementing Marketing-led Strategic Change', *European Journal of Marketing*, 24 (2), pp. 24–42.

———— (1992) *Market-led Strategic Change*, Oxford: Butterworth-Heinemann.

Piercy, N. and Giles, W. (1989) 'Making SWOT Analysis Work', *Marketing Intelligence and Planning*, 7 (5), pp. 5–7.

Porter, M.E. (1979) 'How Competitive Forces Shape Strategy', *Harvard Business Review*, March–April, pp. 137–45.

———— (1980) *Competitive Strategy: Techniques for Analyzing Industries and Competitors*, New York: Free Press.

———— (1985) *Competitive Advantage: Creating and Sustaining Superior Performance*, New York: Free Press.

Quain, W. and Jarboe, G.R. (1993) *The Marketing Plan Project Manual*, St Paul, MN: West.

Ries, A. and Trout, J. (1986a) *Marketing Warfare*, New York: McGraw-Hill.

———— (1986b) *Positioning: The Battle for Your Mind*, New York: Warner Books.

Robinson, S.J.Q., Hichens, R.E. and Wade, D.P. (1978) 'The Directional Policy Matrix – Tool for Strategic Planning', *Long Range Planning*, 11 (3) (June), pp. 8–15.

Saunders, J. (1991) 'Marketing and Competitive Success', in M. Baker (ed.),

The Marketing Book, Oxford: Butterworth-Heinemann.

Suidan, Z.M. (1994) 'Ten Commandments for Marketing Planning', *Marketing News*, 20 (20), pp. 4–5.

Sun Tzu (1981) *The Art of War*, London: Hodder and Stoughton.

Tull, D.S. and Hawkins, D.I. (1990) *Marketing Research*, New York: Macmillan.

Verhage, B. and Waarts, E. (1988) 'Marketing Planning for Improved Performance: a Comparative Analysis', *International Marketing Review*, summer, pp. 20–30.

Webster, F.E. (1991) *Industrial Marketing Strategy*, New York: J. Wiley.

Weihrich, H. (1982) 'The Tows Matrix: A Tool for Situational Analysis', *Long Range Planning*, 15 (2), pp. 54–66.

Wensley, R. (1981) 'Strategic Marketing: Betas, Boxes, or Basics', *Journal of Marketing*, 45, summer, pp. 173–82.

Wild, R. (1984) *Production and Operations Management*, Eastbourne: Holt, Rinehard and Winston.

Zinkham, G.M. and Pereira, A. (1994) 'An Overview of Marketing Strategy and Planning', *International Journal of Research in Marketing*, 11 (3), pp. 185–218.

Index